Paths of Heart
Writing Stories Told at Life's End

A Memoir by
Richard Haverlack

OffRamp Books
Allison Park, PA

For me there is only the traveling on paths that have heart,
on any path that may have heart,
and the only worthwhile challenge is to traverse its full length.
And there I travel, looking, looking breathlessly.

don Juan Matus

.

CONTENTS

Dedication

The stories in this book are those of real people who were in the care of the Good Samaritan Hospice. This book is dedicated to those gracious people who, at the ends of their lives, took their superlatively valuable time and spent some of it telling me stories they wanted others to hear. Because I cannot now ask them for permission to use their real names, I have used pseudonyms in the text of this book. However, here I would like to acknowledge, in no particular order, the real people whose stories are related in some measure in *Paths of Heart*.

Virginia McMillen
Hazel DeVinney
Albert Croskey
Irene Andrews
Georgie Butler
Shirley Phipps
David Shaner
Joseph Scholl
Ruth Musser

There are no composites in this book. All of the characters are real and all the action is either from audio recordings made during my interviews, memoirs written by me for the patients, or my best recollection. People appearing in this book who were not hospice patients have each been made aware that they appear and given a chance to read what I have written. Their real names are used herein.

Note that the last person on the list above is bit different—she was not in hospice care, but I wrote her memoir as I did the others. She has seen what I wrote and approves.

Ruth Musser graciously agreed to be the pilot for this kind of writing—she was the pioneer through which I aligned my sights and set my methods.

To the journey of writing Ruth's story, as with each and every other story in this book: I am hopefully the wiser, but oh so much the richer, for having taken it with her.

-RH
February 15, 2018

Journey: Prologue

In the Oakland Veterans Administration Hospital of Pittsburgh, Walter Haverlack lay in his bed, comatose, helpless. Having served in the Marines, and then being called up again into the Navy of World War II, he was doubly qualified to be in this hospital. Near death, he was also qualified to get one of the few private rooms.

He'd been a pretty tough guy, making a good living as a journeyman firebrick layer. Until his lung cancer made itself known, he'd never been sick. Even after surgery, trying to do the demanding physical labor of his profession with only one lung, he'd never complained. But at last he'd finally been flattened by our culture's double whammy: disease and the treatment for it.

While my father lay there unconscious, 3,700 miles away in Sydenham, England, St. Christopher's, the world's first hospice, was coming into its second year of operation. Back in the United States, however, the word *hospice* had not yet entered the popular lexicon. The first U.S. hospice would not open for another five years. And it would take more than thirty years for the American Board of Medical Specialists to finally formally list hospice care as an approved treatment regimen.

Of course, back in 1969, when we were so terribly anxious about Dad, we knew nothing of this. What we knew was that Dad needed help.

I was having a lot of trouble dealing with the situation. I was in the middle of a master's degree in engineering at a nearby university, and my father was hospitalized with brain cancer. For the two months plus that he was in the VA hospital, I'd attend classes, do reading and homework and thesis research, and then I'd fit in a visit to Dad's bedside. I was turning in the worst grades of my academic life.

I saw Dad's situation as hopeless from the first visit to our family physician. We insisted he go after he'd become disoriented and stumbled at my undergraduate graduation party in April. He'd wanted to shrug it off, but my mother, sister and I insisted we visit the doctor the next day. That wise, kindly man did not have good news. He felt that Dad's lung cancer had most likely metastasized to his brain. Since I knew the doctor as well as one of his patients could, I read more into his somber intonation than the words he spoke. The message was clear to me: It was fatal.

But that was not the last of the diagnoses. We put Dad into the hospital and got him "the best neurosurgeon in Pittsburgh," according to our family physician. After an angiogram, that man told us he thought Dad had had a stroke. We were all so relieved.

That was early in May.

By September, when I returned home from Army basic training in Georgia, it was clear that Dad was deteriorating. His confusion and his shuffling gate were worsening. No longer able to afford the hospital, we got him into the veterans hospital. There, his diagnosis had come quickly.

Dad's lung cancer had in fact metastasized to his brain. The tumor, now large, grew deep inside. "Probably fatal," we were told. I noted that doctors were careful never to make a definitive statement—always to leave some doubt, some hope. In contrast, my own career training dealt *only* with the definitive. There is not much room for gray in the black and white world of electronic engineering. However, with the confirmation of our family physician's words back in May, I knew my father was going to die.

But in September Dad was not yet totally debilitated. He could walk, talk, eat and even occasionally laugh. They had to *do* something, didn't they?

Led by my mother and sister, and with my own opinion held in check, that demand — plea, really — was what the doctors heard.

So Dad was scheduled for surgery for his brain tumor. The outcome, they said, was "doubtful." I think that meant something different for me than it did for the rest of my family. They took it as signal of hope. I took it as one of hopelessness. But it didn't matter either way. Dad never had the surgery.

Minutes before the surgeons were to open his head, while descending into anesthesia, Dad had his first heart attack. The surgery was canceled, and the surgery option was withdrawn because of the newly increased risk of another heart attack.

Still, they had to *do* something, my family entreated.

That was when radiation was discussed. The doctors were even more doubtful, but they said it was the only thing left they knew to try. In 1969, chemotherapy was not yet even to the clinical research stage.

But at least radiation was *something*.

Dad had the treatment. As the doctors had warned might happen, the X-rays swelled his brain. Dad descended into coma.

Something had been done, all right.

Now the doctors all agreed, and said so: "Nothing more can be done." Back then, all the medical profession knew to do was to try to heal through various treatments. When there were no more treatments to try, that was it. Hospice was not yet an option to consider. With the pronouncement of "Nothing more can be done," all that remained was to helplessly watch and wait.

For my mother, my sister, and me, their final pronouncement was a kind of relief. We need not feel guilty any longer. We had done everything that could be done. Even though the doctors had been careful never to be positive about any of the treatments, urging them to try anyway was all we could think to do. The only alternative would have been to sit and wait. I admit that I, too, share the blame for what had happened. Our insistence on treatment had actually made Dad worse.

So with his final fate soon and certain, family and friends made their last visits to my comatose father. Mom, my sister, and I could only watch and wait, taking turns to come to the hospital and sit by Dad in his stark, sterile hospital room.

Inevitably, on November 8, 1969, Walter Haverlack paid the ultimate price for his two-pack-a-day Camel cigarette habit. He died at the young age of 53. He'd had his cancerous lung removed from his body two years earlier. The die was cast then, really.

I was 21. Gone forever was any opportunity for Dad and me to become man-to-man peers. That is a void I still have found no way to fill.

I finished out the term, but dropped my merit fellowship and left the university for full-time work. I did what I had to. Citing fine print in Dad's life insurance policy, the company refused to pay the considerable medical expenses of his last public hospital stay. I'd gotten Dad into the VA hospital as a last resort, but older bills still had to be paid.

Even now I'm conflicted about how things might have been in those last six months had we never been given the false hope that came with stroke diagnosis. I know we would have done a lot of things differently had we faced Dad's dying sooner, rather than as late as possible. But what Dad would have wanted, we will never know. Although he was wise enough to know that it was more than a distant possibility, neither he nor anyone else in the family ever broached the topic of death.

* * *

It would be forty years before my next close-up experience with death. Even though you would think given that much time I'd be better prepared, I wasn't. Absolutely no less confused, frustrated, and guilt-ridden, I did my best to muddle through. And my dislike of the iffy nature of medical treatment hadn't improved either.

Even so, the events surrounding that second intimate death would ultimately introduce me to one of the most rewarding things I've ever done in my life. It would bring me to the work of writing memoirs for hospice patients. And the incredible experiences I had in doing that intimate writing is what brought me to create this book.

Six of my stories of writing those memoirs are included here. They are set apart with "A Writing Partner's Tale" in the heading. I don't like to use the words "hospice patient" except when necessary. Those words can give the wrong image of the people I've worked with, implying people who are helpless and dejected and maybe in despair. But that could not be further from the truth of the situation, as you will see.

However, the account of how I came to write for hospice patients in the first place is what this book's main chapters are about. In those stories, hospice itself is something that I would be forced to learn about. Although it hadn't yet been an option back when my Dad died, it certainly was when I next endured the death of a loved one.

If you already understand hospice, you know that it is not a place. It is a mindset, a regimen, and it is the best way to minister to someone who is dying. Its mission is nothing like those of hospitals and the professionals you encounter within them. Hospitals are all about doing whatever it may take to make you well again, to heal you. That is their reason for being. And in some sense *death* is viewed as a failure in that mission.

But hospice has a totally different mission. For the patient, only palliative care is practiced—care that is for treating pain and easing discomfort but not aimed at curing the cause. And in hospice, lovingly sustaining life as it ebbs into death is only part of the mission. Just as importantly, hospice also does the crucial and meaningful work of supporting the family and friends of the patient before, during, and after the death of their loved one. As a volunteer with my writing work, I am part of both of these aspects of hospice care. I get to know my writing partners and frequently their family as well.

I think it is certain that if someone is dying, hospice care—whether administered at home or in an in-patient unit—is undoubtedly what both the patient and their family will opt for, *if* they know about it and understand it.

My main motivation in writing this book is to evangelize hospice to those who read it. I want to persuade readers to learn about hospice before inevitable circumstances force them to make decisions about it. The times those decisions must be made are most stress-filled moments of any life—that is, the moments a life is drawing to a close. Hopefully my tale of how, when and where I came to learn about hospice is one you can avoid repeating.

But the stories of my writing experiences themselves are no less valuable, I think. That's why I've included a few of them here for you. Working with each of my writing partners on their personal memoirs has expanded my understanding of life in ways I could never imagine. Some of the lessons I've been taught, we all could stand to benefit from.

As I work with a writing partner, I try to find their essence. I use this central quality of their personality to flavor their memoir—make it sound like them to familiar readers. Those central qualities are parts of the titles of the story chapters in this book. For me, with the formality of my engineering career, engaging people in such a deeply emotional way has proven to be a very different kind of learning experience.

With tongue just slightly in cheek, one friend characterized the change in, well, personality that I've undergone in doing my hospice work like this: "Now you've become a *high functioning* introvert."

As the opening epigraph of this book hints, I have found that each of my writing projects has been a path of heart.

And following any path of heart, the traveler should never be surprised to experience deeply personal revelation.

A Writing Partner's Tale: *Epiphany*

Every revelation rightly understood and acted upon
clears the way for a higher one.
Anonymous

Epiphany is defined as a moment of sudden revelation with significant insight. We all experience such lucid moments, but only on rare occasions. However, once we do, it etches our memory forever. An epiphany recalled springs into our mind full-blown and vibrant, filling our senses, just like it was happening again. Epiphanies are amazing. But for most of us, sadly, the flash of epiphany is extraordinarily uncommon.

Peter Innes had a mission he wanted me to continue for him. He had discovered a reliable way to have epiphanies at will, and he wanted to let others in on his discovery. Since I had worked with several writing partners before I met Peter, I thought I had a good idea about how things would go. I was not prepared for Peter, however. He was nearer to death than anyone else I've worked with, before or since. But that grim fact was not what took me by surprise.

It was the intensity with which Peter told his story, the blinding intensity that he mustered to overcome his physical deterioration.

It was the intensity of Peter's intensity, really, that taught me how to cry again.

Like Peter Innes, if asked, I can vividly describe my most significant personal epiphany without hesitation.

When I was a young working professional just about to turn thirty, I thought of myself as well traveled. I'd been all over the country on business and on vacations. Today the phrase would be, "Been there. Done that." So when three friends decided to go on a two-week European vacation, I pooh-poohed the idea. Why would anyone want to travel that far when there were plenty of cities and countryside to see right here? They are all pretty much alike, no? I didn't see the attraction, so I simply declined. I thought that was the end of it.

But one of the fellows had to drop out. All of his tickets were already bought and paid for. Airfare and a two-week Eurail pass—it came to quite a sum. So more to help a friend out of a financial jam than anything else, I reluctantly agreed to buy his travel arrangements. After all, I had a good job, and he didn't. And the timing—early autumn, my favorite season—was right for a vacation.

So armed only with Arthur Frommer's original *Europe on $10 a Day*, off we went.

Looking back, I now see that what happened was inevitable. We landed in Luxembourg and spent the day walking around jetlagged, with a free street map for a guide. I'd read nothing to prepare me. I didn't think there would be anything to prepare *for*.

But simply in wandering around, street by timeworn street, my amazement grew. Narrow, cobbled pavement. An 800-year-old cathedral, built before Columbus sailed. Old men playing chess in a coffee shop. Back then, Starbucks was just a single shop in Seattle, still unknown in the rest of America, much less the world. Europe had had coffee shops since the 1600s.

The food smelled different. The food looked different. The food *tasted* different. Even the beer was different, really different. Micro-brewing was still decades in America's future. With a palate cultivated at fraternity keg parties, I thought Budweiser was beer. But the stuff I drank in Luxembourg that first day in Europe was, well, more beery. Just plain tastier. And the money. The train. The hotel. *The people.* People on the street dressed different. They spoke language — languages — I didn't understand.

Epiphany had at once opened my mind to the world. And it taught me to value rather than dismiss international travel, taking every opportunity to extend international business trips and spend vacations abroad. That fellow who had turned down (and almost missed out on) an opportunity to take his first trip to Europe simply vanished that first afternoon. The one who replaced him has experienced dozens of places, from Shannon to Sydney, Athens to Auckland. Cities on the beaten path like Cairo and Paris, even Moscow at the height of the Cold War. And tiny towns not on most people's paths, like Haast in New Zealand and Stranrare in Scotland—places no one except locals has ever heard of. I even chose to live abroad at the first opportunity, in the picturesque Georgian city of Bath in England.

I trace my appreciation of the world's rich diversity to that one, single, blindingly bright afternoon of revelation in Luxembourg.

That's the lasting impact epiphany can have.

So when Peter Innes—closer to death than either of us realized—told me that he'd had an experience that changed his life, I listened closely. And when he told me what he wanted me to do about it—no, *implored* me—I was deeply affected. When someone so near death can muster that kind of insistence, it deserves all your attention.

When Peter described his first epiphany, it was like watching him travel back to where and when the memory was made. He was animated, arms moving expansively to show scale, voice rising and quickening with excitement of discovery, and the story rushing and tumbling out of him as he strove to keep up with the vivid memory. All this despite lying in a cranked-up hospice bed, breathing oxygen through a face mask.

I was in the Good Samaritan Hospice house in Wexford, Pennsylvania. But Peter was somewhere else. Eyes shut. Traveling through space and time and describing his revelation.

I took down Peter's story on three blustery afternoons as winter was dragging on toward spring. My time with Peter was to be the shortest I'd spend with any patient writing partner for two reasons. First, Peter knew well the story that he wanted to tell. His recounting had been polished over many repetitions. Second, his metastasized bladder cancer was to claim his life in a few short weeks—just days before I finished and printed his story.

Even though he could not even rise from his bed, Peter was one of the most spirited writing partners I've worked with. And his aim was as clear as the stories he told. With me, he spent some of his last hours as an irrepressible evangelist who wanted nothing more than to persuade—seduce, really—others to have epiphanies. And he knew how.

* * *

Peter Innes was a straight-talking man of the earth.

Born into a farm family, he naturally took up the yoke. He owned and operated a working farm, raising much of his family's meat and produce.

"The potatoes. Your own homegrown meat. Your own home-canned fruits and vegetables," he said. "Everything didn't come from the supermarket. It has flavor. It has taste, but no chemicals." He took immense satisfaction from having provided for the welfare of his family in such a direct, personal way.

Peter made another kind of living off the earth—or maybe I should say *within* the earth. He started his own business as a backhoe tractor for hire. Peter dug into the earth for others.

For example, he maintained a contract to dig the graves at a Jewish cemetery. And he kept his mind as well as his eyes open while he waited respectfully for the graveside services to be completed so he could finish his work.

"They would come to visit, and some would still have the ink mark numbers on their arms, tattoos. Holocaust survivors. So it actually happened. One of the blackest moments of our history." His observations became part of him. Peter took things to heart.

"Peter, you've done an awful lot in life. In a few words, how would you describe yourself?"

"I graduated from high school in 1954. I married Janet in 1965."

"Why'd you take such a long time?"

Grinning, Peter was quick to reply. "Oh, yeah. Oh, yeah. I was very bashful. I didn't have any social life at all, except with my friend Bob. That was my future wife's cousin. He introduced me to my wife. He said, 'You need a nice girl. I know one.' And I never looked back.

"I proposed several times. It took Janet a while to get up the nerve. And she finally said yes."

Together they built their own house—with their own hands, not through contractors or hired help. Peter scavenged some of the materials — rafters from an ancient building being razed, window glass from an office building undergoing renovation. When it came to scavenging, Peter was in a class alone.

"I watched the newspapers. I was in a position that I could do it. I mean, what in the world is anybody else going to do with this stuff? What are you going to do with 70 plate glass windows? What's the average person going to do with them? All I knew, I wanted those windows. Figured out what to do with them later."

To hear Peter tell it, that was all building a home took—that and an awful lot of sweat.

After a brief, inexpensive road-trip honeymoon, that was it for travel for nearly twenty years. Peter and Janet settled in on the farm north of Pittsburgh and went to work. Peter ran his backhoe business—ever self-effacing, he openly joked that he was just a ditch digger—tended the farm, had three kids, and simply kept to the business of life with no frills.

"What about recreation? You know, travel, vacations, trips?"

"After the honeymoon, we kind of settled down and went back to work. We took the kids to the Butler Fair each year. That was our biggie, other than our honeymoon, of course ... And we took the kids to Lake Arthur for fishing in the summertime. I always seemed to find a place where we could donate time to the kids. That would be the word, *donate*. Pretty much, we just wanted to stay at home and work. And I read a lot, too.

"And up until we got the gift, we never did anything spectacular."

"The gift" was the real beginning of Peter's story.

As it happened, on the particular frigid morning when Peter told me about the gift, David, his oldest son, came into Peter's room. We made our introductions, and David said he'd come out because he knew I was working with his dad on writing a story. I'd become used to a family's curiosity about my work with their kin.

So I resumed my seat next to Peter's bed, and David sat at the foot of it. I thought to involve David. Sometimes this helps in getting detail.

"David, I was just about to ask your dad a question. Peter, what was that about a gift?"

Although he had not heard Peter's first mention of any gift, David spoke up instead. And he told his story with well-worn ease as well.

"It was for Christmas in 1986. We'd [Peter and Janet's children] already decided what we wanted to get them. So we went to the bookstore and found a book of national parks. Because we didn't know anything about national parks, we just looked for a picture that we liked. And right there in that bookstore, we all agreed, 'All right, let's send them here.' We bought the book, too. Then we went out and booked them a tour at a travel agent so that they couldn't refuse it because it was already bought and paid for. They had to go. We used the tickets as a bookmark in that national parks book, right where we were sending them, and we wrapped it up. That was our only Christmas gift to them that year. Just that one present package."

Unable to contain himself, Peter interrupted David's description, to make sure that I wouldn't miss a key detail: "They were teenagers, get this! They were teenagers and they had teenagers' income…

"I said, 'You can't do this!' But they had done it. These kids were just teenagers. They didn't have any money, and I still to this day don't know where they found the money."

"So where did they send you, Peter?"

Eyes fixed on each other, father and son answered in unison.

"Yellowstone National Park."

My breath caught.

I have been there. And let me say that folks who have not seen Yellowstone are the poorer for it.

Yellowstone was America's first national park. What's more, it was the *whole world's* first. The very concept of a national park was created specifically to preserve the wonders of Yellowstone.

It was established by an act of Congress at the direction of President Ulysses S. Grant in 1872. Yellowstone Territory was so exceptional that a nation not yet recovered from a wrenching Civil War created extraordinary legislation to protect it.

The park is a global treasure too. Shortly after the United Nations instituted the designation of "UN World Heritage Site," Yellowstone became one. There are only twenty-three UN World Heritage Sites in the United States, and Yellowstone was the first. To underscore the significance of this, Stonehenge, the 4,000-year-old iconic English megalith, became a World Heritage site eight years *after* Yellowstone.

So in randomly choosing Yellowstone, the Innes children had picked what many consider the ultimate collection of natural wonders in North America, if not the globe.

From the book they'd been given, Peter and Janet knew there was a big experience coming up for them at Yellowstone. I shook my head to clear the flood of Yellowstone memories and got back to the interview.

"Yellowstone! Wow. And you'd never seen any of the natural wonders back east either. It must have been a shock, the size of everything."

"Oh, yes. Oh, yes. But we had a big shock before we got there, even. That first night we stayed in Great Falls, Montana, and I'm sure of that because that afternoon before we got there they said we were going to stop down here and see Charlie Russell's museum."

Charles M. Russell is known as "the cowboy artist" because he was a cowboy and so were many of his subjects. He'd even illustrated some of the Zane Grey books of Peter's childhood.

Peter explained that he'd never considered art before, but *this* art, art that celebrated the west of his childhood imagination, awoke something in him. In a way, it was a preview of what was to come when he and Janet got to Yellowstone the next day. Those experiences made a lifelong collector of western art out of Peter.

"We had never heard of Charlie Russell. But Charlie Russell turned out to be a turning place in my life, really. I began then and there to actually appreciate real art."

Later I did a little research. To dismiss any notion that Russell's was quaint "folk art," in 2005 his painting *The Piegans* (a Montana Blackfoot Indian tribe) sold at auction for $5.6 million.

Peter stopped to take deep drafts through his oxygen mask.

"Take it easy, Peter. Take your time."

He ignored me. "Naturally I had to tell everybody I knew about it. I had never seen anything like that! Unexpected. Totally unexpected. Oh, yes. Oh, yes."

If I ever get to Yellowstone again, I will take the time to visit Great Falls and the C.M. Russell Museum. Such was the power that the recollection of it brought to Peter Innes on a winter's afternoon more than twenty years after he had visited it.

Peter had been touched. Of course, that is exactly what good art is supposed to do. Even so, the experience was dwarfed by the experience of Yellowstone itself, which began the next day with Peter and Janet's arrival at the park's North Entrance near Gardiner, Montana. In our next interview, Peter related the story he insisted that I had to tell others.

This time, we were alone, and I didn't even get a chance to sit down. Peter was off.

"The first thing we saw in Yellowstone was Mammoth Hot Springs. This mineral water running down over the mountain and it solidified into these tabletops and troughs."

The famous Terraces of Minerva, I realized.

"I thought it was a miracle! But I'd never heard of it. It was another miracle for me, like the museum. The formations looked like a cave in places, but they weren't underground, they were right there on top of the ground. It smelled like sulfur, very strong, very strong. But there again, it was out in the open. There was a walkway around and over the hot spring mineral formations. You could actually walk over the bubbling, steaming water that was making those formations.

"Thank God that somebody had enough sense to preserve all that ... Everybody needs to go see it! ... What they saved for us. Oh, yes. Oh, yes!

"We did take a lot of pictures. Our camera was just a little simple Kodak. It was something I could just click and shoot, none of that jazzy stuff which I still don't understand. It worked, and we took dozens and dozens of pictures."

As an introduction to Yellowstone National Park, Mammoth Hot Springs was perfect. It did for Peter what it had done for me on my first visit. For us both it was a sight we could not have conjured—beyond imagination. Entering Yellowstone Park from the north makes it immediately clear that you've left behind the realm of the ordinary.

Peter and Janet were not alone on their journey of discovery. They were with a tour group of more than twenty people. A natural storyteller, Peter peopled his tales with characters—mainly to show their reactions and buoy his story with the voices of others.

One of those on the tour became the foil for the message Peter was pressing to get across to me—and to anyone who might read his memoir. Many people I've written for are initially uncertain just what they want their memoir to communicate to their readers. Peter knew from the beginning. And so in his storytelling, Peter told about a fellow as an example of what *not* to do.

"And then there was Gilbert. He was a man that just waited too long to come out here... He was a professor of psychology of some sort at the top of his field. He had been teaching psychology in Washington, D.C.

"He waited until he was too old to go on this tour. His health had given out. I mean, he would have enjoyed it much more if he had gone ten years before that. I would guess that he was in his eighties. He just waited too long. But I'm glad for Gilbert that he had the nerve to do it, to come out there, even in his wheelchair. He loved it all, but it was just too hard on him. He had just waited too long."

How long would you have waited, Peter, had it not been for your kids' gift?

Shaking his head to clear it of Gilbert, Peter went on: "That night they took us to Yellowstone Lake. We stayed there overnight in a cabin. We got up early, like five o'clock in the morning, before anybody else got up. Janet and I were walking along the lake and saw these buffalo just sleeping there like you see cows sleeping around here ... And we walked right past the buffalo. And they didn't think anything of us. It was still a dream for us back then. It was still a dream that I was actually *there*."

Not all of the sights that impressed Peter in Yellowstone were natural ones. When most people hear the words "Old Faithful" they think of a gushing geyser. Peter gushed about the Old Faithful Inn. I worried about his breathing.

"Take it easy, Peter. You'll just tire yourself out."

But there was no calming the man. He was on a roll. For a fellow who had built his own house, The Old Faithful Inn, the largest log building in the world, must have been a wonder beyond wonders. It was completed by men working without machines. They finished in 1904.

"This lodge was over seven hundred feet long. I mean it was huge. Old Faithful [geyser] is actually really close."

"[Upon entering] I stood back in awe, as anybody would. I stood back in awe because I had never seen *anything* like this before. Three days before, I just got off a train from the modern world. And here they set me down in the middle of this. It was amazing. It was obvious that it would stay there forever ...

"You can't prepare for that. You have never seen anything like it. And we actually slept in that huge lodge. You can't even describe this. Not only the lodge, but the accommodations that came with it. We slept in a room, and as you can imagine, this room was built in the late 1800s."

Peter's stories consisted of surprise followed by surprise as he relived his and Janet's Christmas gift trip. So I expected him to segue into what was right out in front of the Old Faithful Inn. But I was wrong. The world's most famous geyser? Peter did not even bring it up.

Peter had already known about the geyser, but not about the inn.

I got it then. Peter wasn't recounting a travelogue of his trip. Peter was telling only stories about revelations.

And like any seasoned storyteller, he saved the best for last.

Peter explained that while rest of their tour group was socializing and strolling around Old Faithful geyser, he and Janet were on their way to yet another unexpected discovery. For the two of them it was to be the seminal event of their entire trip, and the memory of it was so vivid that they would use the event as sort of a code in the future whenever they wanted to reaffirm that the world is indeed full of wonder. Peter sobered with the memory of this experience.

Reverence now.

His eyes close, relishing the memory. Peter's voice softens.

"We had the afternoon off to ourselves. We could do what we wanted. Most of the group just hung around and watched Old

Faithful. [But] my wife and I were not very 'people people,' if you know what I mean. And anyway, once you saw one eruption, that was it.

"We wanted to see what else was there rather than the people, too. So we asked [the tour guide] and he told us to go see the Morning Glory Pool, which was quite a hike, as I can remember. Well, we went to see the Morning Glory Pool, and we were never sorry.

"That was..." Peter pauses, at a loss for words for the first time.

"It was so breathtakingly *blue.*" A tear rolls down his cheek.

"From all of the minerals that are in it... Aaahh, look at me..."

Peter takes a few breaths before going on.

"We always come back to that... Remember the Morning Glory Pool. I remember it still today."

Peter pauses again, not out of breath, but eyes still closed, caught up in his memory.

I wait silently for him to return.

"Today we still say, *'Remember* the Morning Glory Pool.' It brought such a... a... contrast to our ordinary lives. Even now today when times get tough... Like here. What's happening to me right now... We say, 'Remember the Morning Glory Pool.'"

Drawing deeply on his oxygen, Peter opens his eyes again. With a tissue, he wipes his cheek.

I lay my hand gently on his.

Now, as a hospice volunteer, I'd been trained not to touch patients without first asking if that was OK. But my mind isn't on my training at that moment. And my mind is on neither the majesty of Yellowstone nor how blue a blue can be. No, I'm consumed with the simple sincerity of this man who lay before me. The earnestness of his story. The depth of emotion in his recall.

For the first time in long years, I need to take out my handkerchief to dab my own tears.

Slowly Peter returns, our snifflings and the hiss of the oxygen the only sounds in his room. He draws another deep draft and picks up his story once more.

"And then we went back to the inn. And the guide had reserved a special table in the inn restaurant. He singled us out and we ate supper with him. He was familiar. He knew."

Yes, the guide *knew*. He knew the Morning Glory Pool would live on and on, vivid in Peter's and Janet's minds. And it has. Right up to that moment. Right there in the Good Samaritan Hospice house.

Even though I've been to Yellowstone, I have not seen the dazzling blue of The Morning Glory Pool. And with Peter's reverent recounting, how could I not put it on my personal list of paramount things I want to do? I don't like the term "bucket list." Those words trivialize what is, for me at least, an important and sobering sentiment: Though longer than those of the hospice patients I work with, my days too, are numbered. And I've important things yet to do and see. Things like just how blue a blue can really be.

Peter wanted the stories of his memoir to awaken others, the readers of our writing. He felt that if he could just *get them out there,* readers would have their own epiphanies. He closed out our last interview, the very last conversation I would ever have with him, with what can only be called a plea. I chose to put his words into his memoir as a direct call to action

"We're pretty much at the end of our time today, Peter. How about if you tell me how you would like to close out your story?"

"As I said, each sight was amazingly different from the last. Everything was just so different from what I was used to from the very beginning to the very end. It was an awakening to me. And it can be for *you* too."

Turning his head on the pillow, Peter faced me directly.

"Hey! There's a more amazing world out there than what you've been living in. There's a *different* world. You need to go see this world. You need to go show your children this world.

"Back at that stage of the game I thought that there's no guarantee that this will always be here. Sure, the government said that it'll always be here, but I guess at that time, I didn't believe that it would always be here.

"Time is wasting. Don't be like Gilbert. Don't wait until it's too late. Do it now. I say you have to show your children that these things are here. You have to go see it."

Peter' eyes widened as he said these things. I knew his urging had dual meaning: He wanted *me* to get the message, but he also wanted to speak to whoever might read his memoir, too. As he lay there, days from the end of his life, he wanted to urge people to *get out there and make epiphanies happen!*

Peter didn't mean to limit his words. He was speaking to anyone who could hear. He was speaking to anyone who would read his memoir. He was speaking to all of us.

* * *

From the first moments I spent listening to Peter tell his story, I knew there was something about him, about his attitude, about his storytelling that seemed eerily familiar. It took a while, but out of the dim past it finally came to me.

Back in the 1970s there were a series of controversial books written by an anthropology student from UCLA. For the work framed by the books, Carlos Castaneda was awarded a Ph.D. The books became extremely popular, and Castaneda even rose to the pinnacle of American popular culture, capturing the cover of *Time* magazine.

Castaneda did his field research living among the Yaqui Indians of northern Mexico. He wrote extensively about their culture in general and their spiritual beliefs and deep connection to nature in particular. In his writings, Castaneda is apprenticed to a Yaqui shaman, a teacher and spiritual leader whose name is don Juan Matus.

In meeting Peter Innes, a specific memory of a specific passage came to me.

Carlos Castaneda begins *his* first book, *The Teachings of don Juan: A Yaqui Way of Knowledge*, with this translation of a quotation from don Juan:

For me there is only the traveling on the paths that have heart, on any path that may have heart. There I travel, and the only worthwhile challenge is to traverse its full length.

And there I travel, looking, looking breathlessly.

* * *

My delivery of Peter's memoir, which I'd entitled *Remember the Morning Glory Pool*, to his grieving family at the funeral home was not the end of Peter's story.

Since he had died before he could read what I wrote for him, I could not know whether Peter would think it genuine. I felt that I'd captured him and his voice, but I would never have his opinion on the matter. Writing for people in hospice, I know that death can come at any time. But Peter Innes's departure was doubly sad because he'd not seen his story in print.

A week after I'd given Peter's memoir to Janet and their children, I got a phone call from Peter's daughter. She said that as a profound thank-you, the family wanted to pay me for my work. They had all read it, and they declared it to be astonishingly (her word, not mine) faithful to the events and attitudes it described. As always when such a thing occurs, I was grateful for the gesture and affirmation, but as a matter of principle, I will not accept payment for writing the stories of dying people. I consider the privilege of being taken into the confidence of a person at the end of their life and entrusted to carry forth what message they would choose to be reward enough. On the phone, I gently said as much.

In the mail three days later I received this note: "Our Dad, Peter Innes, had only a short time with you. However, the work and kindness you have given our family and his memory are immeasurable. You gave Dad great joy in listening to his stories, and I know that you shared many of Dad's passions for the National Parks. You are a great man as was our Dad … We miss him… In appreciation, please accept this gift." And there, enclosed with the note written by Peter's eldest son, was a sizeable gift certificate to a national chain bookstore.

As I held the gift card in my hand, it was not lost on me that on a Christmas day long ago, Peter's children had given him a gift that he could not refuse—one that had been bought and paid for and one that would be wasted if he did not use it.

It had worked once, so they had done it again.

Shaking my head, but with a smile on my face, I thought: *What would Peter do?*

Peter would want to continue evangelizing America's great treasure, her national parks. After his Yellowstone experience, Peter had traveled to most of them, from Alaska to Arizona, continually having epiphanies begun with a Christmas gift. And he'd advocated the experiences to anyone would listen, telling them point-blank to get out there themselves. I simply had been the last in a long chain of listeners.

So I thought to continue his crusade.

I used that gift card to buy two copies of a large-format, coffee table book—a fantastic photographic tour of all of America's national parks. I placed a copy of the book on the coffee table in the living room of each Good Samaritan Hospice in-patient unit—the one Peter was in, in Wexford, Pennsylvania, and the other in Cabot, Pennsylvania. The living rooms offer a place where family and friends visiting a hospice patient can go to decompress and relax.

When I was in one of the hospices several years later, the book I'd left was still there, well worn, frayed with use.

Peter would be delighted to see this.

Inside the front cover of each of each book, I had pasted a notice for the reader.

"This book is placed here at the Good Samaritan Hospice in memory of Peter Innes who was a patient here. As you appreciate the magnificent photographs in this book, Peter has something he would like to tell you about America's natural wonders:

'My wife and I were there, and people just roll their eyes when I start about it. They know what's coming—that they have to go see these sights before they die.

Because *you* have to go see Yellowstone. *You* have to go see the Grand Canyon. *You* have to see the redwood trees. *You* have to go see Alaska.

You have to! You have to do that!

After seeing Yellowstone, I wanted to get to as much of the North American Continent as I could see. And I wanted to be in a position to say that I was there to see it all.

But you need to go too!

And if you get me started, I'll go on about it forever…'"

I'm not sure there is an afterlife, but if there is, I know what Peter Innes is doing there. He's talking to anyone who will listen, and I know about what. And I also know one more thing.

Peter thought he had discovered a matchless way to ensure that he might have an epiphany—a journey of discovery of self as much as anything else. And although I agree that travel, to a national park or to any other destination not yet experienced, is a wonderful way to such revelation, it is not the *only* way. For me, a much more reliable and rewarding way to experience the deep insight of self-discovery is simply to listen to the story of another, any other. Like, say, a self-described ditch-digger. Just really listen.

Journey: Sustaining Frank

I suppose you could say I'm not too big on groupthink—even when the group consists of only a few.

I prefer situations where I can act independently. I don't mind at all the extra responsibility that comes with acting alone. And I especially don't miss the debate that comes before anything is done in the first place.

When my father was dying, I tried to stay out of the discussion for his treatment as much as I could. But sometimes it was impossible: "Well, what do you think, Ricky?" I was well aware that, as the youngest of the family, and still in university, I was being drawn in more for my mother's and sister's need for affirmation than for my opinion. It was polite to ask me. And it was polite to agree with them as well. But I knew that Dad was going to die. And soon.

In 1969, cancer was a death sentence, given the state of oncology of that day. No matter what would be done, the outcome would be no less certain. The tumor that was growing in his brain, metastasized from the cancerous lung he'd had removed almost three years earlier, would claim him, sure and certain.

I'd said my goodbye to Dad weeks earlier. After class one sunny September afternoon, I'd come to the hospital alone, and I sat next to him as he lay on his side in bed. The brain tumor had claimed his speech, but not yet his cognition.

As my father looked silently at his son, his eyes completed the message sent by the gentle squeeze of my hand in his. It was all right. He knew what was happening to him, and it was all right. And he saw that I knew, as well. And that was all right, too.

Over the coming weeks, I got directly involved in Dad's treatment decisions only when I could not avoid it. And really, with most family matters, that was how I operated—how I wanted to operate. Trying to convince the family of the futility that I saw in Dad's treatment options was not something I felt up to. Dash their slender hopes? Not me. But given that the radiation treatment I tacitly agreed to probably hastened his death, I was culpable anyway. Sins of omission, and all that.

So it should come as no surprise that when the time came years later, I acted the same in dealing with Dad's youngest brother, Frank.

Frank Piasecky was Dad's half-brother, really, but that distinction was never in evidence. The two men were best friends, sharing a trait of incisive intellectual capability that belied their levels of education. And they shared a taste for Jack Daniel's whisky as well. When they got together, naturally, spirited debate was no stranger to them. Whether the topic du jour was the Cold War or Socrates (though neither got beyond public school they had both read Plato's *Dialogues*), they would challenge and expand each other's thinking.

When it came, Frank appeared to take Dad's death as well as one could expect. But given that the two of them had also shared the stoic's mien, it was hard for me to tell for sure.

As I matured, slowly but steadily, I seemed to slide into a relationship a lot like Dad's with Frank. When I'd visit him, we'd invariably wind up in one geopolitical debate or another. And yes, Jack Daniel's was still involved. I didn't visit him as often, but when I did, I think Frank enjoyed my company as much as he had my father's.

Frank Piasecky was a loner. I'm not sure if this was by choice or by habit, but it certainly was his dominant characteristic. Frank had worked all of his life as a mail sorter in the main Pittsburgh branch of the U.S. Postal Service. He had never even bothered to learn to drive—living in the Pittsburgh urban neighborhood of Lawrenceville, he didn't need to. His job was just a few streetcar stops away. He never married, preferring to live with and care for his immigrant father, my grandfather, Dominick. But even his bachelorhood was not the most prominent feature of Frank's isolation.

Frank preferred to work the night shift.

Frank would awaken in the early evening. Make dinner for himself and Dominick. Read a little. Maybe translate a letter to his father from the Old Country or write one back. Like all of his siblings, Frank was American-born, but he had taught himself to speak, read and write Ukrainian so that he could correspond with his father's family. Dominick's brothers and sister were all trapped behind the Iron Curtain. It was the chilliest time of the Cold War.

Corresponding in Ukrainian was but one testament to Frank's academic nature. Even though he only finished high school, he was able to learn that language by piecing together conversation with his illiterate father with reference books from his local public library. To do so, he had to learn the Cyrillic alphabet as well.

So while Pittsburgh prepared for bed, perhaps with a Ukrainian letter to ponder over his lunch, Frank would arrive at the post office to sort the mail the city would receive the next day. And at mail sorting, Frank was very good. So good, in fact, that he was offered promotions to management several times. All these offers he turned down. When I learned of this some years later, I breached our usual protocol and asked him a personal question: Why?

"I didn't want the responsibility. Other workers had to be constantly watched and frequently disciplined. I did not want to have to do such things. The extra money was not worth the aggravation—at least not to me." When I mentioned that mail sorting had to be mind-numbing, Frank showed his different way of being once more. "Well, I took it as mental challenge—a chance to exercise my memory."

Over the years he had memorized the names and addresses of all of the corporations and the mail routes for the entire business district of Pittsburgh—his assigned territory. That way, without the need to look anything up, he could sort the mail in a fraction of the time others took. Naturally, his territory was then increased, but he didn't mind. He had to be there for eight hours anyway, he reasoned, so why not be busy? In those days of zero-sum unionism, Frank's outlook did not win him admiration from his co-workers.

Like me in my early years, Frank stayed close to the familiar. Indeed, while his father was alive, he never traveled anywhere. I knew that he had served in India during World War II, although he never had much to say about it.

But when his father died and he retired from the post office, overnight Frank morphed into a world traveler. It's clear to me that it was the need—the responsibility—to care for his father that had kept Frank close to home. Being an intellectual, he wanted to see firsthand some of what he had read about. And once he felt free to travel, he did exactly that. All by himself, Frank took trips to Israel, and back to India where he had been during the war. He traveled to Egypt and to the Ukraine and even up the Amazon before the travel industry made such trips into package deals. He was not a conventional tourist, either. For instance, he took no photos. And he preferred to research, then explore the places he visited on his own, giving guided groups wide birth. Later, when I discovered the delight of travel myself, I thought of Frank. Perhaps we shared a gene for travel of a certain in-depth kind—the antithesis of "Been there. Done that. Got the T-shirt."

So whenever Frank would return from a trip, I'd always show up interested in hearing about his journey. But he was not much of a storyteller. He gave concrete descriptions with only a few of the feeling words that personalize most people's tales. In marked contrast to how he held forth on political debate, for details of his trips, you needed to ask direct questions.

I was especially interested in his trip to the Ukraine. He'd been writing to family there for years. But beyond a description of the primitiveness outside of Kiev and the malaise that Communism seemed to have brought to the country, I got nothing from him about how he felt when he traveled to his father's homeland.

Then, when things in Frank's life seemed to be just as he wanted them, bridging one trip to the next with research, everything changed in an instant. I learned he was in the hospital.

When I visited him there, he said he fell and severely injured his ankle. As I learned from others later, that much was true. But there was more to the story than just a stumble.

As I've said, Frank was very politically opinionated. His views were extremely—some would say radically—conservative. Throughout the '60s and '70s, he got the national newspaper of the John Birch Society, for instance. He didn't hide this fact, and he was not shy about expressing his political views, especially if a little alcohol was involved.

At the height of our country's union movement, Frank lived in a solidly Democratic, working-class neighborhood. Frank's conservative views of current events were different from his neighbors, to say the least. So the story goes that on the night he hurt himself, he'd had a dustup over politics at a local bar.

Of course Frank, with his high intellectual capacity and broad reading habits, was more than a verbal match for an entire tavern-full of working class opposition. And with an evening's worth of alcohol to neutralize his customary inhibition, it was easy for him to make his fellow debaters look very inferior. That is the nicest way I can put it.

In any event, I was told that Frank had to flee the tavern with several adversaries in hot pursuit. To escape, he leapt over a low concrete wall. But unknown to him, the street on the other side of the wall was much lower than his takeoff point. So the jump was higher than he expected and he severely injured his ankle when he hit. Since he kept himself in top physical condition, the alcohol was probably to blame.

Frank escaped, but even with time, his injured ankle never healed properly. And as frequently happens with people beyond their prime, decrease in mobility was the first domino in a downward spiral.

Sadly, travel was now out of the question. And Frank could not exercise as he always had. So his whole physical condition began to suffer. Even walking the several blocks to his beloved library was now a real chore.

To compensate for his mobility problems, Frank relocated for the first time in his life. He left the Lawrenceville section of Pittsburgh for East Liberty. He moved into a large apartment building that had, as its main attraction, a supermarket right across the street. That the supermarket was open twenty-four/seven probably clinched the deal for him. Through decades of habit, Frank still preferred the night. Now, able to return to the side of the clock that was most comfortable, Frank became even more reclusive.

About that time, without saying a word of it (at least to me), Frank gave up alcohol. He just did it. He had done the same with cigarettes many years before. "Will power" is not much talked about these days, but as I see it, when Frank abandoned his vices, that was all he used. And of course he did it alone.

Inevitably, withdrawing from the daylight world and losing his physicality took their toll on Frank. His personal hygiene declined. And his previously meticulous tidiness gave way to a disheveled apartment. His diet moved more and more to convenience foods. I watched all this with increasing alarm, yet I did nothing to help him. In my own introspective way I reasoned logically that *he* should be the one to act, even though he meant a lot to me.

By today's standards, my family of eastern European heritage was close knit. Even so, I was especially drawn to Uncle Frank. When I was young and somewhat of a weakling, he bought me a complete set of free weights. Beyond simply giving a gift, he wrote out a daily lifting program similar to his own for me. Then, when I was showing academic promise in school, he bought me vocabulary workbooks. It was what he had used to stimulate his intellect, he said. And I must say that, although others may claim to be interested in words, to this day Frank remains the only person I have ever known who actually owned a personal copy of the entire *Unabridged Oxford Dictionary of the English Language*—all dozen or so huge volumes occupying some four feet on his bookshelf above his set of the classics. Now *that's* an interest in words.

Earlier, he'd given me a chemistry set. Then there was a gift subscription to *National Geographic,* and a near-professional globe one Christmas. Frank was fundamental in sparking my own enjoyment in learning, I am certain.

Ashamedly thinking back on it, with all he'd done for me, I know I should have confronted Frank when he needed it. But biased to avoid personal confrontation, I reasoned Frank's situation was his business. I reasoned he should be the one to realize what his needs were and to act accordingly. At least that reasoning was the wall of logic I retreated behind as things slowly deteriorated. Oh, I did make one fumbling attempt to lift his spirits and refresh his interest in learning things: Thinking his curiosity could be rekindled in the emerging online world, I convinced him to buy a personal computer. As I installed it for him, I thought—hoped, really—that it might bring him out of his increasingly dark funk.

I tried to train him on how to use the computer and the Internet, but in the 1990s the arcane things he had to do to connect and to make his way around the digital world were daunting. Looking back, I see that I had unreasonable expectations. Frank had never operated anything more complex than a TV set—and the one he'd still owned did not even have a remote control.

So it came to pass that although I should have been the one to help Frank to address his own deterioration, I was not. Even though he had overcome alcohol and tobacco alone, Frank could not summon the will to prevail when it was his own body that was failing him.

* * *

As I closed out his lease, Frank's apartment building manager told me that some of the residents called him "The Count." As in Count Dracula. His preference for the night side had been more excessive than I'd thought.

I had become Frank's guardian, not by choice, but out of necessity. Frank, now in his eighties, was in assisted living. And I'd not had anything to do with getting him there.

To her lasting credit, my cousin Rose Mary Haverlack had not been not so reticent as I about confronting Frank's declining physical and mental condition. She had become increasingly alarmed, too, and we had talked about it on the phone a couple of times. But I wasn't much help to her, I'm afraid. So she decided to act on her own.

On an otherwise nondescript day, Rose Mary took charge. A spunky woman with assertiveness honed by years of teaching in Pittsburgh's inner-city schools, Rose Mary simply showed up at Frank's apartment, told him to put on his coat, escorted him to her car, and drove off to look at assisted living facilities. Just as brusquely, after the visits she squarely confronted Frank and announced: "Pick one. You're moving—*now.*"

Faced with Rose Mary's determination, and probably realizing his own decline, Frank did as he was told. To preclude backsliding, she drove him once more to the residence he had chosen and accompanied him back inside. She sat him down at the manager's desk, asked for a residence contract, and handed Frank a pen. Given no room to hesitate, he signed. With any dithering averted, Frank was moving into a new, and somewhat up-market, assisted living facility.

Rose Mary had given him no other choice, really, but he did not protest. She did the right thing. He knew it. We all knew it. Maybe he had been waiting for something like that to happen all along. Maybe I should have been the one to do it. But I hadn't.

Once the deciding part was out of the way, once all that remained was a long checklist of necessary actions, I swung into motion. I helped Frank to move, to terminate his lease, to downsize, and to get what he needed for his new place as well as to reassign addresses and inform all those who needed to know. It wasn't the work or even the responsibility that I'd been avoiding. It never was. It was the need for confrontation.

Even though he had let himself go, Frank Piasecky did not suffer from dementia. As it was later explained to me, what he had was chronic depression. And moving to a new place was the best thing that could have happened to him.

The residence Rose Mary had shepherded him into was a new facility and quite attractive. The residents came from broad backgrounds—from doctors to truck-drivers—and so it had some diversity, which was good for Frank. I didn't think he was antisocial—since he'd retired, he'd just been used to being a loner. That had been OK when he was able to be independent, but now he needed others to help him. I was delighted with the way things were working out, even though I'd played no role in bringing it about.

Rose Mary was friends with the receptionist at Frank's center, and so she could get sub-rosa updates on how he was adapting. Of course, when asked directly, never one to complain, Frank would invariable say that everything was fine, so getting an independent assessment of his situation was simply wonderful.

Then, too, Frank's assisted living facility being in the suburbs, I was closer to him, making it easier to visit more frequently, which would become important with time, as things turned out.

Thankfully, Frank seemed to be improving. Residents ate communally, and were actively monitored to ensure that they were getting to meals—he could no longer hole up in his apartment. And Frank's medications were administered so he could not fail to remember to take them. He had a number of ailments, chiefly his depression, but nothing life-threatening. And now that he was more or less forced to socialize, he seemed to be actually making new friends. The staff had set him up at a dining table with several other World War Two veterans. And the scuttlebutt was that he got on well with them. I was delighted at this news.

Rose Mary, who had insisted Frank move, had decided to follow her own sister's lead and retire to Florida. So I started visiting Frank more frequently. But that was not the only consequence of Rose Mary's relocation.

Years earlier, out of the clear blue, Frank had decided that I would be the executor of his will, a move that seemed to have as much to do with my interest in him as my ability.

Even though I might not be very good at initiating things—especially in a negotiated environment—when I accept a responsibility, I take it seriously. So I'd suggested Frank also create a living will and a healthcare power of attorney. For these, too, he decided that I was to be the named responsible person.

With all that, it was inescapably logical that when Rose Mary moved to Florida, I was the one to whom the guardianship of Frank squarely came. This was not a legal guardianship, but a desire that Frank had to have someone else manage his affairs, even though he was mentally capable of doing so himself. So I dug in, opening joint accounts and consolidating his finances, which were predictably in a mess. I did long-range spreadsheet planning for him to show that he could actually afford the managed care center where he was living—putting to rest his worries about insolvency. We both breathed easier knowing everything was under control.

Things were finally getting better for Frank from every point of view.

Rose Mary still got sub-rosa reports from her friend, and she passed them on to me. Frank was socializing. With friends, he would take the facility bus to go to the supermarket to buy fruit to keep in his room and personal necessities. Once more he was always clean-shaven, barbered, and neatly dressed. He continued his newspaper subscription and increased his reading and studying activities.

Just as important as where he now lived, Frank seemed well liked by others. One afternoon he told me a personal story. A female resident had asked him to her apartment to help with hanging a picture. He agreed, and went up the next morning after breakfast. But once he got in her place, the woman made it clear that she was hoping for more than just a picture-hanging. He said he beat a hasty retreat.

That brought a smile to my face, but really, it was another story that brought outright laughter. Frank, himself, never mentioned "The Employee of the Month Award" lark, as I was fond of calling it. The story came via cousin Rose Mary and her spy.

Frank and his table-mates cooked this up all on their own—it was nothing that had ever been done at Frank's facility before. Once a month these fellows would jointly decide who their very own Employee of the Month would be. They would award the successful caregiver with a box of expensive chocolates purchased just for the occasion. And they came up with a bit of a ceremony to present the award—no point in keeping an incentive program a secret!

When I heard this story, I laughed out loud at the thought of Frank and his new friends publicly awarding their chocolate. Obviously or not, they were openly inviting all the other caregivers to compete in serving them. Brilliant.

Then, with trips to see local high school plays and even an invitation to me to attend the Veterans Day event he participated in, I came to believe that Frank was at last on his way to a social and enjoyable old age. Compared to his long years of solitude, I felt Frank was living a personal revelation of sorts.

I breathed a lot easier.

* * *

One sunny summer afternoon I got a call from Frank's assisted living center. He had been sent to the hospital emergency room. Over the course of the two years he had been at his residence, he had had to go to the hospital several times, including a stay for his depression. This time, however, he was ambulanced for a new, unexpected reason. I got as much detail on the phone as I could before heading for the hospital. He'd had an accident, I was told. But I wanted to know exactly what had happened.

"Well, as you know they have their big meal, their dinner, at midday. And at dinner, Frank started choking on his food. When he began to turn blue, one of the aides tried the Heimlich maneuver, but he couldn't clear it, so we had to call the ambulance."

As I sped off to the emergency room, I began to understand why on many of my visits to Frank's residence I'd seen an ambulance there, just arriving or just leaving. With older people, many infirm, hospital and emergency room trips must have been frequent. Increasingly, with Frank, I was becoming a part of that emergency medical picture, no longer outside looking in.

When I got down to the hospital, I was told that they had taken Frank up to the gastro-intestinal lab. They'd X-rayed him immediately and discovered his esophagus was packed solid with food. They were "working on him" now. Worried, I took a seat and waited until the doctor finally came for me. I leapt to my feet.

"He's OK now, but he's had quite a time. In my whole career, his impaction was the largest I've ever had to clear. His entire esophagus was packed with food. It was really something—whole florets of broccoli even." Shaking his head, "It was really something."

"Will he be OK? Can he to go back to his residence?"

"Oh, yes, but there may be a complication. With this kind of impaction, if food got over into his trachea, his breathing tube, it could cause trouble in his lungs. There's no way to know if that happened."

I got Frank checked out of the hospital, a process that always seems to take hours. He sat by silently, looking a little sheepish as I avoided talking to him about what had happened. Really, I was more worried than angry. But I wanted to wait until we got back in his own room to talk. I finished up the paperwork and drove him home.

When he was back in his own bed, I pulled up a straight-backed chair, sat and studied him. He looked haggard and shamefaced at once.

"Want to tell me what happened?" I asked.

"Well, I was having trouble with my false teeth—they were hurting me."

"Oh, so you had trouble chewing?"

"Ah… Yes. I took them out."

"You took them out? Right there in the middle of your dinner?"

"Ah… No. I'd taken them out before I went down to the dining room."

"You went down to dinner without your teeth? What were they serving?"

"Roast beef."

"What?! You tried to eat a roast beef dinner without your *teeth*?"

He looked away toward the window, cowed. I'd never shouted at him before. "Uh, yeah. I guess it was pretty dumb. But the teeth really were hurting. I thought I could cut the food up in small pieces and be OK. Then when it got stuck, I tried to force it down with more food. I really am sorry that I had to inconvenience everyone, you especially."

I softened at his woefulness. After all, it was just like him—try to go it alone. Solve your own problems. He'd done just that for most of his life, having no one to depend on. So he'd tried his own way. What could I say? I turned toward the practical.

"Oh, well. Let's have a look at those teeth."

"They're over there in the top dresser drawer"

The chair scraped on the polished floor as I got up, went to his built-in dresser, and pulled open the top drawer. The teeth were lying there on a paper towel, and in a single second, I saw they were not right. Literally every tooth, in both uppers and lowers, was worn flat halfway down to the pink plastic gums.

(Sigh.)

"Frank, how long have these been like this? And when's the last time you were to the dentist?"

When he'd first moved to assisted living, I'd had to take Frank to an optometrist. I'd had some papers for him to sign as I was consolidating his finances, and at his desk, he'd taken off his glasses and hunched way over, squinting to see what he was doing. Earlier, I'd noticed a magnifying glass next to his bed. I should have taken a clue from that, but within a week Frank had new bifocals. He'd told me he'd not been to an optometrist for more than ten years. His whole eye prescription had changed a lot. They were amazed he was using his old glasses.

So for the teeth, I was expecting some explanation like that. Back when I was worrying about his eyes, I wish I'd worried about his dentistry too.

"I don't remember," he said.

"Come on. About when?"

"I never went back after I got this pair."

"Come on… When?"

"Well, maybe twenty or thirty years."

Now I knew why they were worn flat. But you couldn't tell when they were in his mouth. So no one knew about it but Frank himself.

(Sigh.)

"I'll get you an appointment with my dentist so we can get new ones that fit better too, OK?"

Ever compliant when being led, "Ah, OK. I guess that's a good idea."

But before we could get to the dentist, I was called to the hospital emergency room yet again.

This time Frank was having serious trouble breathing. He had developed something called aspiration pneumonia. As the gastroenterologist had warned might have happened, some of the food particles from his impaction episode had gotten into his lungs, causing infection and swelling them with fluid.

Frank had to be admitted to the hospital for his pneumonia. It was pernicious. They had a hard time trying to clear it up. He was hospitalized for two weeks. Eventually they got it under control with antibiotics and inhalation therapy.

But amazingly, even though you might think professionals in a hospital would know better, while they worked hard to clear Frank's lungs, they simply let him stay in bed all day. There was no reason for him to get up or to walk around. And in his semi-depressed state, Frank had no desire to do so either. He no longer had to get to the dining room for meals, or to his mailbox for his newspaper. Everything came to *him* in the hospital. It was something that hadn't occurred to me, and it seems the staff hadn't thought about it either. So when it came time for Frank to be discharged, he couldn't walk. His legs had atrophied.

With that news, Frank's residence would not let him come back—people who lived there had to be ambulatory. They insisted that he go first to a nursing home for the physical therapy he now needed.

I followed the ambulance there and got Frank admitted. It was a grim place with sad-looking people in beds and in wheelchairs. No one except the staff seemed to be walking under their own power. However, they managed to get Frank walking again, albeit with a walker. We both were glad to be leaving that thoroughly depressing place.

Unfortunately, his nursing home stay had a totally unexpected and lasting impact on Frank. Because the staff there had been informed of his food impaction episode, they had made notes in his record that he required a special diet and someone to supervise him when he ate. Usually such supervision is reserved for patients with severe dementia. Of course with Frank, it wasn't dementia but ill-fitting false teeth that were to blame. Nonetheless, supervised eating had been prescribed for Frank at the nursing home. Naturally, he had not mentioned the supervised eating to me. And just as naturally, it was indelibly on his record. Although he was far from it, he was marked with a requirement usually reserved for those unable to even feed themselves.

But I knew nothing of this as I prepared to get Frank back to his pleasant assisted living center.

I called to tell the place we would be coming in that afternoon. My call was transferred from one person to another until I finally was talking to the manager. He told me that they (to whom) I had been writing a $3,500 check every month for a couple of years) now had to refuse to take him back.

I was told that they'd been faxed Frank's records, and that his food requirements now "exceeded their level of care." I argued about how that eating supervision note had come to be put on his record, but I got nowhere. The nursing home "diagnosis" was there in black and white, and only a lengthy medical evaluation could remove it. While I was trying to appeal, on several levels, the nursing home contacted me to inform us that Frank must leave. His Medicare coverage for their kind of services was running out.

I had to get Frank out of the nursing home, but we had nowhere to go. I was given two days do something. I needed to act, and fast.

Luckily I found an agent to search through all of the assisted living places and find one that was not full and that could meet Frank's "level of care," requirement as bogus as it seemed. I reasoned that once things quieted down and I got Frank a new set of false teeth, we could try again for a better residence. The place that now accepted him was clean and well maintained, and the staff seemed capable, but the residents were clearly much more infirm than those of Frank's previous place. There was even an occasional whiff of urine in the halls and lounge. More than that, though, I was worried that without the stimulation of companionship Frank would drift back into his isolated ways.

But I had a plan, and first things first... The dentist and the false teeth.

I made an appointment with my dentist, but we never got there. I thought I knew what needed to be done, and I envisioned how to do it. As an engineer and product manager, I'd been making much more complicated analyses and plans my whole career. But I was jumping to an unwarranted conclusion about Frank. I should not have been so certain about his condition.

A Writing Partner's Tale: *Bliss*

Working is so satisfying that if we didn't have to work to eat,
we'd have to invent some other reason for doing it.
Andy Rooney

I try not to set any personal expectations before I begin writing with a newly assigned hospice patient. I've learned that it is impossible to guess what a person will want to talk about. I've also learned that whatever it will be, it will be unique, so there is simply no point in anticipating.

But as I drove north to meet the oldest person I have ever known, cruising along on a sunny-crisp autumn afternoon, I just could not help myself.

I was on my way to the Concordia elder residence complex near the tiny town of Cabot, Pennsylvania, to meet Alice Wiggins. When I worked on her memoir, Alice was 106 and counting. To provide some perspective, she was born when Roosevelt was president, and that would be Theodore, not Franklin. Alice came into the world before the Panama Canal, and shortly after the Wright brothers' first flight.

Alice had to have seen an *awful* lot.

Dazzled by the thought, I gave in to my imagination and started to think ahead to the story I would write. As I steered hard right onto Marwood Road, I realized that Alice had experienced the dawn of the automobile era. How had she gotten around before it? I pulled into the parking lot and clicked off the car radio. How would she describe the advent of radio? She would have been just entering her teens. And, *oh my,* Alice was born even before widespread electricity distribution! Having worked in several technology arenas, I knew there was a long, long list of marvelous inventions Alice witnessed coming into the world. What stories would she tell of the arrivals such things? How had they affected her life? What did she first think of them then? How about now?

I grabbed my notebook, made sure my recorder was in my pocket and stepped out.

As I made for the entrance, again I could not keep my thoughts in the present moment. Alice had lived during a lot of what we all know as *history.* She had lived through both world wars from start to finish. She was born more than a decade before the Soviet Union came into being and had outlived it by more than that. She had lived through eighteen presidents. How would she see the modern ones we all have known and the misadventures we can easily list?

As I grasped the doorknob an autumn breeze blew cool, yet the sun warmed my back. Change of season was in the air. Maybe too, change in the kinds of hospice patient memoirs I'd been writing for five years. The sheer potential of the stories Alice was certain to tell me would bring it, I thought. This memoir was *really* going to be very, very different.

I was right. But my reasoning was all wrong.

I knocked at Alice's slightly ajar door and went into the spacious, double occupancy room. To the left sitting in a rocking chair was a woman in a pressed floral blouse and slacks. She didn't look to be 106. The she saw me, waved a little wave, and with eyes and head motioned toward the other side of the large room, divided by a floor to ceiling curtain. She must be Jean, Alice's roommate. I nodded to her, and she smiled back. I walked around the curtain.

There sat another woman, who did not look old enough either. She sat just to one side of her bed in an easy chair, her lap draped with a knitted afghan. Dressed comfortably in a housedress and a cardigan, this *must* be my next writing partner.

"Alice?" I ventured.

The woman looked up from her well-worn Bible and gave a single curt nod. Peering over her glasses, her gray eyes regarded me matter-of-factly. Her long, smooth fingers slowly closed the Bible. With her uncreased face held slightly tilted, she said, "You must be the writer fellow."

"Guilty as charged," I joked.

It went nowhere. I sobered, cleared my throat.

"If it's OK, I'll sit down and maybe we can talk."

Alice gestured to a straight-backed chair that seemed to have been placed there for me.

"Alice, my name's Richard and I'd like to tell you about what I hope we can accomplish together."

Alice listened silently as I proposed how we would work together to create her memoir. Along the way, as I always do, I took the tiny digital recorder out and showed it to her as I explained I'd have to record our interviews. Beyond a glance, Alice gave it little attention, even though others much younger had marveled at the tiny size that belies the device's considerable capabilities. Though the gadget got little notice, Alice's focus sharpened as I pulled out a copy of a past memoir. I explained I had written it for another patient, but that Alice's own would look like it when we were finished. She took it from me, eyes curious. She leafed through it, one page at a time—not reading, but gauging the breadth of it. "It's a lot bigger than I thought it would be." As she held that memoir, I think she was assessing whether I would be able to capture what she had to tell me. Her circumspection was prescient, as it turned out. Alice's stories wound up taking more than 14,000 words.

Still holding the document, Alice looked up slowly and steadied her unclouded eyes on me. She was taking my measure. After several seconds of consideration, with an almost imperceptible nod, Alice signaled her decision. Both the memoir and its producer had passed muster. Alice Wiggins decided to go ahead with the writer fellow.

* * *

In the coming weeks, I learned what sorts of stories Alice wanted to tell. With consistency and earnestness, she told me what to write for her. My initial musings could not have been further from the mark.

Take history, for instance. I'd been sure that Alice would provide a great retrospective on events that had shaped the last hundred years. After all, she had lived through it, and so much of it was so interesting—to me, anyway.

I could not have been more wrong about what the woman considered important. "History" was the basis of just one of her many stories: Alice made a point of telling me she had been born in Grafton, West Virginia, which was also the birthplace of Mother's Day. She was eight years old when President Woodrow Wilson came to Grafton to launch the new national holiday. But in summing up the momentous occasion, Alice simply said of Wilson, "He looked a little pompous." That was it. He looked a little pompous.

Even the two world wars got no billing in Alice's mind. She simply shrugged off these mind-boggling historical events when I questioned her.

"Those things happed far away and to other people. They never affected us." She was only a teenager during the first war. During the second, her husband, a steelworker, was exempt from the draft, while her son was too young to serve.

Looking at the seemingly younger woman, a thought crossed my mind. We know that stress shortens lifespan. Maybe Alice had discovered something in her lack of concern for things far away. Why worry about things that you couldn't do anything about anyway? Momentarily, my thoughts drifted to our 24/7 news-driven infotainment society. Maybe less would give us more—longer life, that is.

Not wanting to go through a litany of historical event questions, I instead thought ahead. If Alice did not feel that the world wars, the greatest historical events of the twentieth century, were significant, then so be it. Getting her impressions on history would clearly not be a theme of her memoir. I realized that while driving up that first day I'd perhaps jumped to a conclusion, one about what *I* wanted for Alice's memoir. That had been a mistake.

But, still, there was technology. I was certain that Alice would come to talk about the inventions that came into her life as a homemaker and a mother—inventions that simply had to affect her life in a very direct way. How could she not think them important? Another mistake.

Here is but one example of how mistaken my thinking was. Alice talked about her early married years in the purpose-built town of Vandergrift, Pennsylvania. She and her husband moved into the company town, where he worked in its steel mill. Her house was just like all the others. In particular, it was heated with coal. She happened to mention that at one point they replaced the furnace with one that used gas.

As a child, I remember my grandparents' house in the city of Pittsburgh. One of the reasons that place got the name "The Smoky City" was because of the pall in the air—partially from burning coal, not only at the steel mills, but also from the many homes that used coal for heat. From my childhood Christmastime overnight stays, I remember that my grandfather had had to get up every morning to stoke the furnace in the basement to heat the water that ran through the big iron radiators upstairs. He'd start his day shoveling coal at 4:30 a.m. Then the family would have a warm house and hot water when they all awakened. During the day, when he was at work, my grandmother would have to periodically go down and shovel in more coal. By the time I came on the scene, she'd been doing that for more than thirty years. Her family of seven had depended not only on this sort of daily maintenance, but also that of re-ordering and the delivery and storage of the black shiny rocks that made the heat. You did not want to run out of coal.

So when Alice happened to mention her company house heating changeover, I tried to take advantage of the opportunity.

"Alice, my grandparents had coal heating when I was a kid. I remember what it was like for them. You haven't mentioned much about how modern conveniences changed your life, but really, when you switched to gas heat, it must have been a relief to you."

Alice dismissed this notion with no hesitation. "I just took it like everything else," she said. "It came along when we were supposed to have it. It never bothered me that we didn't have things that others did, like radio and TV. I wasn't anxious at all, and I didn't envy those that had them before us."

Well! But still not willing to let the topic of innovation go, my mind raced to think of something that would have had to have been a big deal to Alice. She'd been a homemaker all her life and she had to have seen momentous changes in how she went about her work. Was there a device that would have been indispensable to a full-time homemaker and mother of three?

"Alice, what about the refrigerator? When you were growing up, you said that you didn't have electricity."

I was forgetting just how long Alice had been preparing and storing food. She came up with an answer I never expected.

"When we got it, it was a small thing. The iceman came and put ice in it. Of course you had to empty the [melted] water from underneath that icebox or it would run out over the floor. That was when we lived in Indiana [Pennsylvania]. I was still living with my parents."

Of course! An icebox!

"We also got milk delivered to us after getting the icebox. Before that we had a cow. We used to milk that cow—we just had the one—every day. We weren't such a big family and it seemed that one cow was enough."

A cow for the five children. I hadn't even thought about an "inconvenience" that big.

Then, finally, what I was expecting first came at last.

"Oh, of course later we got an electric refrigerator that you didn't have to put ice into. We got that long after I was married, though. It was an improvement."

What I thought of as a necessity, Alice saw only as an "improvement."

Later, at home going over the day's interview, I scratched my head.

We'd been talking a lot by this time. Hours spent, but I didn't seem to be getting it. Looking over notes and going over recordings, I was getting nothing that heralded Alice's advanced years—nothing that showed what she had lived through. I'd thought that *that*—the things Alice witnessed—would be the theme of her story. But I was wrong.

In looking for Alice's reactions to historical events and to new products, I'd simply not been listening to her empathically. I'd wanted to hear what I wanted to hear. I was not hearing what Alice wanted to tell me.

What I needed to do was not only listen to her stories, but also appreciate what, from her viewpoint, these stories were about—what was important to Alice Wiggins? I went back over the interviews we'd had and listened again. This time I tried not so much listening to what she was saying, but how she said it—the tone and tempo of her voice. And there it was, right where it had been all along. Alice had been telling me what was important to her right from our very first meeting.

Sitting there at my desk in a darkened room, I finally got it: The most important thing in the long life of Alice Wiggins—all she really wanted to talk about—was *work*.

And if that were true, why should Alice praise any home product advancement? That is, if you love work—love labor—what, then, is the great benefit of a "labor-saving" device anyway?

As this clear and lucid woman of 106 years sat there in a managed care facility and reminisced, what she longed for, what memories that made her happiest, was purely and simply *work*.

In our next interview, I resolved to help her tell me about it.

"Alice, I've been thinking about the stories you been telling me, and I guess I'm curious about something: What do you remember as your first job?"

Eyes instantly animated, with obvious relish Alice swung right into a story.

"My first job was rowing a boat across the Cheathaven River. I'd take the miners to work. That was during World War I. I was only about twelve.

"I was in fourth or fifth grade when we moved back to West Virginia. We had been in Pennsylvania where my father was working in a glasshouse near Connellsville.

"That was when I started to row across the river. In the morning, early, I'd take the men across, they were working at the mines. If the river was too high, too dangerous, they would row themselves and they always would see to it that I had a boat on my side of the river so that I could get across. They had two boats there.

"I got $25 a month! [Something like a dollar a day.] The mine paid me. They were working real good because of the war and they needed a lot of miners. So I'd row in the morning and then go to school. And I'd come back when they got off. I'll never forget that, I think. That's where I got my first paycheck."

That evening, I decided to do some fact-checking. Sometimes, when a story sounds incredible, I do this just to be sure that the memoir I'm writing doesn't have any gaffes in it. But I could not find a reference to a "Cheathaven River." After World War I, in 1926, a hydroelectric dam was completed across a river that had had various names before that time. That dam formed Cheat Lake. Today a hiking path there still bears the name Cheathaven Trail. It's likely that the riverbed it's named for is now at the bottom of the huge lake.

And then there was the issue of the mine, a business, paying for child labor. Wouldn't it be illegal for a young child to work for actual wages? After some research, I found out that the Supreme Court had struck down the child labor law in 1918. It was not to be replaced until the Fair Labor Standards Act in 1938. So for twenty years child labor was perfectly legal.

Indirectly, I was getting the history I'd wanted in the first place.

Seeing the need for perspective on the changing historical backdrop of Alice's stories, I decided to put a timeline into her memoir as an Appendix. If I could not easily get the context of her stories, it seemed it would be a good idea to help future readers to avoid the predicament as well.

So what else did Alice talk about in our five interviews of more than an hour each? Work. Lots and lots of just pain work. To Alice Wiggins, work was not the background of life. Work *was* life.

Outstanding among Alice's stories of wallpapering, gardening, painting (walls, not canvas) and the like, Alice Wiggins really lit up when she described the labor in life that she relished above all others.

Alice loved to quilt. Work that becomes art. And art that is useful on cold winters' nights.

"Alice, you've mentioned 'quilting' several times. Can you tell me a little about how you did it? I'm afraid that I don't know anything at all about it."

"I used a sewing machine a lot, yes. On many quilts, but not on this one." She gestured toward her bed. "It's all by hand. You used a sewing machine to make the white strips and when you turned them so that the right side was out. Then you had to use a thimble and needle and thread. I used a thimble. I always put it on my middle finger.

"These days, they do embroidery on machines, but what I did on my quilts, it was all by hand. The Amish people used to do all of their quilts by hand, but now even they do a lot on sewing machines, I think."

I took a very close look at Alice's bed covering, which I now understood to be one of her quilts. I had assumed it was printed, it was so raucous in color and pattern, but now I saw it was *sewn*. The quilt had an intricate design with a lot of detail. It was so complex and had so many patterns—literally more than a thousand pieces of cloth, by my quick estimation. There were hundreds of square patches, each sewn into a circle of "ticking" which together formed an interlocking pattern of rings, every one with its own square patch centered in it. The patches were a random rainbow of color. Each was a piece cut from patterned material—a rocking horse in one, a smiley face in another, a bouquet in another and so on. So the quilt was a riot of random color and patterns, and yet the quilt was an orderly array of interconnected circles and squares.

"I finished that one after I came in here. I made the quilting part, a lot of it, at home. Then when I came in here I finished it, I put the binding on it. Long ago I made my son and daughter [each] one like that."

By far the most amazing thing about the quilt on Alice's bed was that she'd created it only four years earlier. She created that quilt when she was 102 years old—by hand.

"I did it. Oh, I really don't know how long it took me to do it. Probably a couple months. I saved up all the material from when I was making dresses and aprons and curtains and pajamas and everything. It's a little bit of everything there. And it's all handmade. Oh, it's a good time-consuming piece of work. I mean, you can sit down and do a little bit of work on it anytime you want to. There's a little bit of everybody's clothes in there. Yes, I just included a little bit of everything. I did a lot of sewing work around the house.

"This was the last one I made, the last quilt I made. And I loved to do it. I always loved to quilt. Oh. I didn't think it was so much. I just loved to do it. I like to get something accomplished. I think I made four like that in all."

Only when I directly asked about it did Alice guess that she had made more than fifty quilts in her hundred-plus years—mostly by hand. Proudly, she described the quilts she sewed, and it was clear that they, and the work that went into them, was, still, very important to her, and making them was a joy of labor. The quilts she had made were for newlyweds and new houses, and for new babies, and even one birthday request from a grandson who travels a lot. That one features the state seal—all fifty of them. I asked, and Alice rather matter-of-factly replied that, yes, she did create each seal from scratch from pictures in a book. I'm sure there's a similar story to each and every quilt Alice has made. But even without hearing all those stories, what came through clearly, with the sparkle in her eyes and gestures of her hands, was Alice's joy in making them. And also the joy they had brought those she gave them to. They were Alice's history. They were her life. And they were a warm and soothing legacy to her loved ones, one beyond what the memoir I was writing with her might ever be, I realized.

Learned at her mother's knee, quilting formed a backdrop for everything else going on in Alice's very busy existence—all the chores of cooking and cleaning and gardening—and all of the things that raising a family and keeping a household would entail. Alice said she always kept a quilt project going and when she would take a break from her housework, she would pick up her current quilt and sew a little more of it into existence. For Alice, quilting was a break from other work—a break from work that was, well, even more enjoyable work. And many of her stories were about that other work too and how fulfilling and meaningful it had been for her.

As I wrote Alice's memoir, I recalled an old saying that some work in order to live while others live in order to work. It seemed to me that Alice saw life and work in a third, simpler way: working is living, and living is working. To Alice Wiggins, these two words are the same thing exactly.

Alice did tell a few stories about things other than work. But really, they were more or less coincidental (and brief) tales of things she'd done. I think she dutifully related them, feeling that they were more or less what I expected to hear. None were told with much detail or excitement.

What *was* memorable for Alice, what she most exuberantly described to me, were loving stories of cleaning and painting and wallpapering and cooking and gardening and sewing and picking berries—stories about activities that few others would enshrine in their memory. Take the annual making of apple butter. Alice described this seasonal event with more than just recollection. With considerable detail, she talked about the several-day process she undertook each and every year when the apples were ready. One day to peel and core them – bushels and bushels of them. The getting ready of the huge cauldron to cook them in—too big for any other purpose. The two-day cooking down—all the while stirring, stirring, stirring. The cooling and then the putting up in dozens of and dozens of Mason jars. While it was the work, or really the joy of it, that she described, she also mentioned the participation of family and friends and the sharing of the apple butter itself. Alice supplied a community with it. She was known for it, back when fresh apples could only be had but once each year.

To Alice, the stories like that one were really descriptions of her life's joys. Her telling of it had the things good storytellers include: all of the senses (the smell of it, the viscous bubbling sounds, the heat of the cauldron, the tasting to see if it was just right). The story began with the bargaining for the apples and ended with the taking of the jars of the newly made butter around to friends and to strangers alike. Alice told it all in the present moment of memory.

Suddenly Alice's face saddened. Turning to face me, she pleaded she wanted *right now* to once again cook apple butter, to cook *anything*. And she wanted to paint and garden and sew. Right now. She wanted to work even at her advanced age, and even though she knew her end was near. As I sat quietly and listened, I saw that all Alice wanted was to be working, working at anything.

When patients repeatedly express the desire for their life to end, the Good Samaritan Hospice adds to their diagnosis sheet the words "failure to thrive." I'd been aware of this assessment of Alice from the outset, but not for the reason behind it. Now it was clear to me.

Without work, why go on?

And at the heart of her lament lay something else. Throughout our hours together, this was to be the only regret Alice ever expressed. As she at last took me into her confidence, I could see it overshadowed everything for her.

Alice turned away and looked out over her quilt made even more vibrant in the slanting sunrays of autumn. "If I could just work with my hands, I'd be so much happier. I'd like to make more quilts. I'd like to make a quilt or *do* something. But I can't here. I can't do anything I used to.

"I've been here longer than I thought I would. It's three years ago in July. I didn't want to come in here. I said I wanted to stay in my own house—to keep taking care of it. That's all I ever wanted to do. That's all that ever made me happy.

"We thought maybe I'd only be here two or three weeks. But now, after so long, how I miss working with my hands."

The only thing that Concordia assisted living does *not* provide for residents is work, and this woman who had lived an uncommonly long life through an amazing era knew that that alone was what she needed to be happy.

It's a lesson that is most profound in its simplicity, I think.

So at the end of Alice's completed memoir, I added this epilogue for her readers:

"The dictionary defines "work" as activity involving mental or physical effort in order to achieve a purpose or result.

But as Alice Wiggins's stories have taught me, there is something that is missing from that definition. It says nothing about what work does to and for the *worker*. And Alice has showed me what that is.

Alice taught me to now recognize something I have personally experienced throughout my own life. But it is something I never tried to put into words before. Not so surprisingly, I experienced it again in working with her and then sitting long hours writing what you now hold in your hands.

Simply put: work well done brings bliss."

Alice Wiggins, unhappy for the first time in her long life, unhappy because she was unable to work, died several months after her memoir of the joys of working was completed. Copies of that memoir, entitled *Bliss,* had been wrapped to give as Christmas gifts to her two surviving children, themselves in their eighties, and to Alice's many grandchildren.

* * *

Some months after Alice's memorial service, I had the good fortune to come across an excellent translation of an ancient book. Had I discovered it earlier, I certainly would have read a short excerpt of *Tao Te Ching* to Alice. For although she knew work to be rewarding, perhaps its own reward, she would have undoubtedly appreciated that this notion is by no means a recent discovery. Written by Lao-Tzu in the time of Confucius (551-479 BC), the book offers this reflection:

> "Fill your bowl to the brim, and it will spill.
> Keep sharpening your knife, and it will blunt.
> Chase after money and power, and your heart will never unclench.
> Care about people's approval, and you will be their prisoner.
> Do your work, then step back.
> The only path to serenity."

I think that if somehow he could read Alice's memoir of a lifetime of joy through work, the ancient philosopher would simply, knowingly, smile and nod.

Journey: Living Will

Things were not going well, but I had a plan. But, as John Lennon wisely said, "Life is what happens when you're busy making other plans." And life was about to demonstrate that to me once again.

Even though he was now in a new residence, the call I got advising me that Frank was being sent to the hospital started the same as all the others. First they assured me he was OK, and then said they were acting on his best behalf. They said that he was having serious trouble breathing and his pulse/ox was dangerously low. Pulse/oxygen is what is measured by a pulse oximeter, that plastic-clip sensor that they put on your finger—it measures the oxygen in your blood while it also takes your pulse. They had already called for an ambulance.

Now wary of the hospital that had let his legs atrophy, I told his new residence manager to tell the ambulance to take Frank to a different one. Then I hung up and raced to its emergency room.

When I got there, Frank was in a triage room, no longer conscious. I fumbled through the emergency admissions paperwork and went to sit with him. Oxygen was being administered through a nose cup.

After a chest X-ray, Frank was admitted to the hospital in order to treat the pneumonia that was once again the culprit. Still unconscious, he was placed in the hospital's Critical Care Unit, which I took to provide care that is somewhere between intensive and whatever regular might be. Here, I was not permitted to stay with him. It was late in the day, so, exhausted, I went home. To eat, worry and try to get some sleep.

When I returned early the next day, I was directed to the chief pulmonologist before seeing Frank. In quiet tones, he told me that Frank was dying—that there was really no sure way to treat his pneumonia. He went on to say that even though he as conscious now, an extended hospital stay over a period of many weeks of rigorous and invasive treatments would be needed and probably would not be fruitful. He finished by saying that even if it was, the pneumonia would most likely return again anyway.

My mind reeled. *All because of his false teeth. Unbelievable!*

I had not been prepared for this. I had a *plan,* for goodness' sake.

Still dazed, I asked to see Frank. We'd have to talk about this.

Upon entering Frank's room, I got a second shock. He was in a cranked-up bed, awake, but with a full-face mask strapped to his head. And he was in restraints—his arms were leashed to the bedrails. Through the mask's transparent faceplate, Frank looked out at me in misery. I had not seen a mask like this except in movies of deep sea divers. It encircled his whole face and was tightly strapped to his head.

A hose led from the mask to a machine at Frank's bedside. The thing looked like many other hospital instruments, finished in neutral beige, peppered with switches, dials and a luminous display. It periodically huffed and chuffed, and each time it did, Frank's chest heaved another breath.

Aghast at the sight, I recalled that Frank had, in his living will, explicitly stated that he wanted NO TUBES (feeding or breathing) to be inserted, no matter what the emergency. He did not want to be artificially sustained, but it did not say that part in words. I had provided this document to the admissions clerk the day before. Because of Frank's visits to emergency rooms over the years, I had learned to bring along not only his living will, but also the document that named me as his healthcare power of attorney.

I could see that in fact they had inserted no tubes. Instead he had an airtight, full-face mask strapped to his head. I learned that the machine it was connected to is called a C-PAP machine, a continuous positive airway pressure machine.

So although he had no tubes, a machine was helping Frank to breathe nonetheless. Written more than ten years ago, the language in Frank's living will had not kept up with the times and the technology. I knew this was not what Frank wanted.

The doctor spoke up, "I'm sorry about the tethers, but Frank tried to take the mask off, so we were forced to restrain him in order that he not harm himself."

Outside Frank's room, the doctor went on to say that Frank had been dazed when he awakened, so they were not sure he knew what he was doing.

Wouldn't <u>anybody</u> *be dazed coming out of an oxygen-starved unconsciousness?*

Instead of pointing that out, I told the doctor Frank was not out of his mind—didn't have dementia—and the restraints should be removed. The doctor hesitated a while. Then he said, "We're not sure, so we can't do that. We need to run some tests before we decide to do anything else."

I tried to explain it to Frank. We were in a sort of limbo; they wanted more tests as the next step, and we had no choice but to comply. When I'd asked, I'd been told that only alternative would be for us to leave the hospital.

Through his woeful distress, seeing my anguish, Frank reluctantly agreed, dejectedly nodding. I stayed with him as long as I could, then drove home. As I did, I realized that I did not know what to do, other than surrender to the situation. Gloomy thoughts—both about Frank and absurd Catch-22 we were in.

Looking back, I can recall that hospice was nowhere on my mind.

I came back the next day, and the next day, and the next, hoping all the while that the situation would resolve. Thankfully, at last that hope held. Inquiring at the nurse's station, on the sixth day of Fran's hospitalization I found the pulmonologist in the glare of the hall outside the CCU. He told me flatly, "The tests show that your uncle's pneumonia situation is even worse than I suspected. His pulse/ox is up sufficiently now, but it would take invasive procedures as I thought to treat his condition. In any event, the probability of recurrence would almost be certain anyway. And as for the C-PAP machine and mask, or better yet a trachea tube, without it your uncle will die within twenty-four hours."

I'd made myself ready for news like this. Although I'd hoped that they could *do* something to make him well, I knew Uncle Frank wanted nothing dramatic to be done.

And somewhere during my sleepless nights, I'd resolved that as Frank's guardian, my duty was to see to it that *his* wishes, not mine, were met. I suppressed my desire to badger the doctor. And it felt very wrong for me not to make him detail all the things that could possibly be done for Frank. But I'd made up my mind that this situation was simply not about what I wanted.

As I look back on it now, standing there in that hallway glare with the doctor's dire prognosis whirling in my head was the *exact minute* when I should have asked that Frank be transferred to a hospice. But since I knew nothing about such a thing, that simply had not occurred to me.

So instead I came up with a plan to at least end the Catch-22. I asked the pulmonologist to accompany me to Frank's bedside.

Frank was still in restraints. Miserably, he looked out of his breathing mask, his chest rising and falling in synch with huff and chuff of the C-PAP machine.

Turning from Frank to the doctor, I said, "Doctor, please assure yourself that Frank is of sound mind."

The pulmonologist looked startled, but perhaps realizing where I was headed, he recovered and turned to face Frank. He bent low so Frank could hear through the mask. He asked Frank a few simple questions about where he was and who he was and how old he was and who George Bush was.

Satisfied, the doctor straightened up. "He's lucid."

Now it was my turn to bend down over Frank and look into his eyes. Weary despair looked back.

"Frank, if this mask is taken off you, you will die in a matter of hours. Do you want us to take it off you?"

Muffled by the mask, Frank nodded and mouthed the single word, "Yes."

I turned to the doctor. He now fully understood that what was happening was going to relieve him of a burden. He again bent low over Frank and said, "If that mask comes off, you'll die. Is that what you want?"

Again Frank nodded and emphatically mouthed, *"YES."*

Wanting to make it clear that he was not making the decision, the doctor straightened up and turned to look directly at me. Knowing fully what I was doing—not wanting it to be so, but knowing that *what I wanted* was not important here—I spoke up loudly.

"He's sane. He's refusing treatment. Take it off."

That was exactly what the doctor wanted: a direct order. Without a further word, he bent down, unfastened and removed the mask, and switched off the machine. In the suddenly silent room, Frank closed his eyes, centered in the red ring the mask seal had left on his face. I'm sure Frank would have sighed, had he been able.

The doctor noted none of this. Satisfied, he was now concentrating on his clipboard as he wrote rapidly. I turned back to face him once more.

"His hands too, please."

"Oh, right." Fumbling the clipboard, the doctor bent to remove the restraints. Eyes still closed, Frank rubbed one, then the other of his chafed wrists.

I was told Frank had to be moved out of the CCU into a regular hospital room. I was surprised at this, because the pulmonologist had not minced words when he'd told me Frank only had a day.

Why disturb a dying man?

But I was told that, since critical care was no longer what Frank needed, he had to leave the CCU. It took two hours to get a room. I stayed with him while we waited, expecting Frank to die at any time.

But he didn't.

Thankfully, neither did he die on the labyrinthine trip as his bed was wheeled up to his new room. I was glad to see that it was a private room. Neither of us would want some stranger looking on as Frank died.

When the nurse left, I looked down at my uncle. He was getting oxygen through a nose cup connected to a wall escutcheon studded with all sorts of connections and controls. This was it, then. The place where Frank would die.

Frank seemed to now be asleep, breathing shallowly but regularly. Relaxing, no longer having to assert myself to ensure that his wishes were met, I was at last overcome. I teared up, glad that we were alone.

Here he was, dying. Uncle Frank. A man who, unlike my other half-dozen uncles, had taken a personal interest my life was about to lose his. I would miss him so much ... In my grief, I sat down in a chair at the foot of his bed, alone in my thoughts save for the hiss of the oxygen.

Frank had spent most of his life alone. I thought about the loneliness he must have endured. But I thought about it in the way one usually does. That is, I thought about what it would have been like for *me*. It would have been intolerable. So in those moments sitting there in his hospital room, I resolved that Frank, having been alone for so long, should not have to die that way. I decided to stay right there with him until his end.

I sat with him through the day. He roused and opened his eyes in the late afternoon. When a dinner arrived for him, I offered to help him to eat, but he refused everything except the strawberry puree dessert. Strawberry pie had always been his favorite sweet. I gave the liquidized fruit to him spoonful by spoonful. I had never fed anyone else, except my father.

After his tray was cleared away, in the early evening, I went out to the nurse's station, and I asked that a rollaway bed be put in the room. I wanted to spend his last night with Frank.

I called the relatives I could reach and told each of Frank's situation and coming end. I asked them to spread the word. Then I opened out the rollaway bed. As exhausted I was, I remember thinking how much worse the last two days had been on Frank. I took my shoes off, swung onto the rollaway and tried to get some sleep.

But periodically throughout the night Frank's breathing would become labored, and the pain of the fluid building in his lungs would bring a soft moan. When it seemed too much for him, I'd get up and go out to the nurses' station to ask that he be given more morphine. It was one of several drugs that had been prescribed when a floor doctor visited Frank in the afternoon.

And that was how Frank and I spent the first of our seven nights in the hospital together. On good nights we might talk a little. More often, though, we each were caught up in our own private vortex of turmoil, punctuated by the visits from various nurses and attendants doing this or that. Filling his water pitcher.

Adjusting his oxygen. Administering a medication. Checking breathing or pulse. Or whatever.

To be charitable to the pulmonologist, it seems Frank was tougher than he had anticipated—a lot tougher. And his hospital time was a challenge for us both.

For instance, on Frank's first morning in his own hospital room, bright and early, a fellow showed up with a breathing therapy machine. He said it would administer antibiotics in the mist it produced. Incredulous, I went immediately out to see the nurse. Why did Frank need antibiotic therapy if he was dying—was in fact already supposed to have died? She consulted the doctor, a different one than had been on the floor yesterday, and the machine was removed.

And, when lunch arrived, Frank didn't want any. But I could not seem to get them to stop sending it.

But most disturbingly, I repeatedly had to go out of Frank's room to find a nurse to give Frank more pain medication. This was a hit-or-miss proposition. It seems that the doctor on the ward had written in Frank's orders, "20 mg of morphine every two hours or as needed." So was it needed or not? Young nurses would come back to the room and—incredibly, it seemed to me—ask a semi-conscious man: "Are you in pain?" Unless he answered in the affirmative, they would say they couldn't give him more until his next scheduled dose. I'd have to argue with them. Experienced nurses would simply administer the injection.

After a few more nights, in the wee hours after Frank had had a particularly severe coughing fit, I got the nurse to medicate him. Bleary-eyed, I walked up the hall, a Styrofoam cup of Sanka in hand. Even though it was the dead of the night, there were moans and monitor beeps and alarm chirps coming out of rooms, and nurses talking in the hall.

A gray-haired nurse at the central station looked up as I passed. She sadly shook her head and said, "It's really tough, isn't it?" I turned toward her in the harsh brighter-than-daylight fluorescent glare and replied.

"No, he had a coughing spell, but now he seems to be sleeping again."

"That's not what I meant. Not on him. It's tough on _you_. That's what I meant."

I hesitated a bit. "It's a lot harder on him, I think. He was supposed to be gone in a few hours. I guess that means now he could die at any time. Does he _have_ to be awakened to take his vital signs throughout the night? And does he _have_ to be turned three times a day? That moving really causes him a great deal of pain. And every time you come in to do the blood pressure, you wake him. Is all that necessary?"

"Well, as a primary nurse, it's our duty to take each patient's vitals when we come on to shift and to turn those who cannot do it themselves in order to prevent bedsores."

"But he's dying! Taking vitals makes no sense—nothing's going to be done about them anyway. And the same with turning him. That only puts him in pain for a while."

She sighed. "I know. But on each shift, each nurse is individually responsible. It's the procedure we have to follow."

The next day I found out that intravenous antibiotics were still among the drugs being administered to Frank. That turned out to be part of the reason for his periodic drifts into incoherence. I sought out the doctor on duty and had them stopped.

The morning after that came the most disgusting event of Frank's hospital stay. Usually, I'd go home just after dawn, take a shower, have breakfast and return to the hospital by late morning. I chose that particular timing for a purpose. Since it appeared that Frank's nurses' schedules were always in flux, I assumed that the best caregivers, being the most experienced ones, probably chose to work the daylight shift, so Frank was in the best of hands while I was gone.

However, this particular morning, I returned a little early and saw Frank's breakfast tray for the first time. It was empty of food.

Frank was asleep, so I went out and asked the nurse about it.

"I was wondering, have you been in Frank's room recently?"

"No, not since I came on shift at six."

"Well, who took his food in to him?"

"The food service person brings the tray, but the orderly, Bob, might have been with him. Bob is really good with the patients. They all seem to like him a lot."

"Know where might I find Bob right now?"

"He's in that first room down the hall."

So I went up to the room and outside waited until he came out from whatever he had been doing.

"Say, I can't help but notice that Frank Piasecky in the room at the end of the hall ate all of his breakfast today. He wouldn't eat for me for days. What happened?"

Pleased to present his expertise, Good-With-Patients Bob gave me a big smile and said brightly, "Well they do need their strength, so I try to get them to eat."

"I haven't had much luck with that. How did you convince him?"

"Oh," With a cheery smile he said, "You know, you'd be surprised, but if you just put it in their mouth, they will always swallow it!"

They will always swallow it. Oh, God.

Whenever I'd asked him, Frank had consistently refused food. I simply nodded, saying nothing to Bob. Instead I reported the incident to the doctor. I heard no more about it, but I never saw Good-With-Patients Bob on Frank's hospital floor again.

And that is the sort of thing that happens a lot in a hospital. After all, the people there are trained to do just one thing: their very best to try to get you well and out of the hospital. It should come as no surprise that when someone is dying—is *supposed* to die—a lot of staff in a hospital simply are not trained in what to do. What Bob did was counterproductive to Frank's wishes. Frank knew what he wanted, and he wanted to die, not build his strength to try to get well. Not only that, but being treated that way undoubtedly made Frank uncomfortable in a number of ways I can only imagine. He'd never said a word to me, though. He probably was worried—rightly, as it turned out—that I would get Good-With-Patients Bob in trouble. No, better to just swallow the unwanted food from the fellow who cheerily roused you. Don't make any fuss.

With its bright lights, constant background noise, and unnecessary treatment practices that themselves caused additional discomfort, or distress or even outright pain, the hospital was a terrible place to die.

Even so, Frank's dying in the hospital went on for two weeks.

The experience gave me a new label. Since I would ask questions and give instructions and carefully keep watch over Frank, one of the nurses said, "Well, you certainly are a great advocate for your uncle!" I knew the word, but I had never thought of myself as one. However, in trying to ensure that Frank was comfortable and keeping well-meaning caregivers from doing anything to cause him discomfort or even pain, I could see that in advocating for Frank, I was advocating *against* his caregivers. The experience left a lasting mark on me. If a relative or friend has to go to the hospital, I always ask if there will be an advocate with them. If not, I offer to go along. In the cacophony that is a modern hospital, it seems that having a watchful advocate is the most prudent thing to do.

My next learning experience in the hospital concerned its social workers. I had thought social workers were usually government employees to help the disadvantaged, usually in poor neighborhoods. But it seems that in a hospital, each patient is assigned to one. I learned of this when I was summoned to Frank's social worker's office one afternoon more than a week after Frank was pronounced terminal. It was the first hint I had that there was such a person for him.

"I'm afraid that your uncle will have to leave. There is nothing we can do for him and he is lingering."

Lingering? People keep trying to heal him and you say he is lingering?

I tried to remain calm. "What do you mean?"

"Well, his health insurance benefits for this kind of hospital stay will expire day after tomorrow."

Oh… So that's what a social worker does in here.

"But where can he go? He's already in a hospital!"

"Well, he must go to a nursing home, or there is always hospice."

Hospice… Now, in the long, long week that my Uncle Frank had been dying, that was the very first time that word was ever mentioned to me. But I really didn't know much about it. On the other hand, I knew about the nursing home Frank had been in.

He'd told me that the care there was terrible and he really was glad to leave the place, so I asked the social worker how we could get Frank into a hospice. It turned out that the hospices would need to send someone out to make their own assessment; their Medicare funding requires that *they* certify that the patient is dying. Apparently the hospital's prognosis is not enough. And maybe I could see why that was, since Frank was *lingering*.

For those who are dying, and their families as well, I think it is a good idea that hospices evaluate prospective patients independently. Hospitals simply seem too hidebound to let someone go—even if they want to go.

So two hospices were called. Both did evaluations. And to my utter amazement, both rejected Frank.

The social worker came to tell me why: "It seems that they cannot accept anyone with a diagnosis of pneumonia. It is specifically not one of the fatal conditions that Medicare accepts for hospice."

Shouldn't you have already known that?

So, seeing no alternative, I had Frank's records faxed back to the nursing home he'd been in. They rejected him as well. I called and they said his level of oxygen exceeded their capacity. I buttonholed a doctor about this and he said. "Well, that flow number was chosen simply because it is the maximum available in the room he's in. We can easily lower it to the number of the nursing home's maximum. It really won't make any difference."

Now I was beginning to see what any engineer could only call the arbitrariness of Frank's situation. So I rethought the whole thing, remembering Frank's laments about how he was treated at the nursing home.

I asked the social worker for the phone numbers of the hospices.

I called them both and said that I would pay for Frank's care myself. They were both nonprofit organizations. And both refused again. It turned out that if they were to take money for their service, they would jeopardize their standing with Medicare. You cannot simply opt into hospice. You can only request evaluation. They decide whom to accept.

Head whirling, I talked to yet another floor doctor. His surname rang a bell, so I asked about it, as an icebreaker. The young man turned out to be the son of someone I'd gone to high school with. I talked about her a little, then: "Doc, about Frank's diagnosis …"

And I explained the situation about the hospice rejections.

"Might it be possible to change Frank's diagnosis to not mention the word 'pneumonia'?"

"Well … Yes. How about 'terminal lung disease'?"

Both hospices accepted Frank once the new paperwork was faxed to them.

Even though I might have been Frank's "advocate," I couldn't help but think that none of this should have fallen to me. With all of the doctors and nurses and social workers responsible for Frank, someone should have known and corrected things.

Now very leery of anything to do with the healthcare system, and still responsible for Frank, I decided I'd better personally visit both hospice facilities. Because of Frank's experience in it, the nursing home would be our last resort.

I still knew nothing about hospice, so I made up a checklist of questions to ask on my visits. They consisted mostly of asking how situations I'd watched develop in the hospital were handled in hospice. That word, hospice, was vague to me. Just what happened there?

Like many still do, I'd thought hospice was exclusively a place for cancer patients to go when they had no more hope. Someplace to go to die. A warehouse of sorts.

Now, needing to make a decision and with time very much of the essence, I was paying the price for not looking into hospice in the past.

A Writing Partner's Tale: *Opportunity*

A wise man will make more of opportunity than he finds.
Francis Bacon

There are tricks that make it easier to answer opportunity's knock, but before I met Harry Phelps I hadn't thought about such a thing much. I guess I just believed that opportunity was something that I had no control over, something that came along and happened *to* me.

Harry Phelps had been a machinist from the Mount Washington district of Pittsburgh. An unpretentious man, he had somehow managed to add "global adventurer" to his crowded resume, I'd been told.

Harry Phelps did not explicitly describe how to, well, *optimize* opportunity, but in the stories he told, it's plain that he did this. His were not stories of exceptional derring-do, or superhuman effort. Actually, some of his stories are the kind that anybody can experience—if only they seize the opportunity.

I wasn't thinking about opportunity as I entered the Rebecca Residence of Concordia Lutheran Ministries near Pittsburgh. I was thinking about Harry Phelps. I knew that he lived there with his second wife, Helen, and that a combination of diabetes, COPD, and congestive heart failure was slowly claiming his life. About to meet the first hospice patient I was going to write with, I was more than a little apprehensive, and the information I'd gotten about Harry's nature didn't help much.

Harry's Good Samaritan Hospice nurse had told me Harry was a busy man—pretty much all the time. Our first meeting proved that to be true. Throughout the hour, he kept looking at his watch. At exactly 11 a.m. Harry said, "I'm sorry. I gotta stop now. It's time for my bridge lesson and I don't want to keep the others waiting."

"Well, I don't want you to either, Harry," I said.

I managed to keep my astonishment to myself. Learning bridge! On second thought, a saying popped into my mind, and I couldn't suppress a chuckle. *The man who is too old to learn probably always was too old to learn.* Being in hospice care apparently was no reason for Harry Phelps to stop learning something new, like, say, how to play bridge.

In our first hour Harry had thoroughly piqued my curiosity. I'd come simply to talk about the process we'd use to gather and write his stories. Harry sat fidgeting. When an aide came in with the week's activity calendar, Harry grabbed the pastel pink sheets and eagerly scanned each page while I talked. I'm not sure he had ever heard the word "multitasking," yet here he was doing it.

I was no longer steering.

"I see we're gonna have duck for dinner on Wednesday. Boy, let me tell you about ducks." Abandoning my plan, I reached down and switched on the recorder.

Go with the flow, I thought.

"Great. Go on, Harry, and you see I'm recording now, don't you?"

"Of course, I see it," he said, perhaps a little impatient. "But listen, here's what I wanted to say: After I retired, we once took a trip to Hong Kong. I got a little bored, so one afternoon, I just got on one of those floating buses they got there. I didn't know where it was going, but I thought I could get back by just backtracking. Well, when it docked, none of the signs were in English any more, and I can't read Chinese. But what the hell. I thought I'd be OK. So I just followed the crowd, and they all got on buses—real buses. So I just picked one and got on it too."

This was in the 1980s. Hong Kong was still a British protectorate. It would not become part of the People's Republic of China until 1997. And that "water bus" had taken Harry from Hong Kong, with dual language signs, to the Chinese mainland. Since only locals used it to get to and from work daily, there probably wasn't much in the way of border control. Although he didn't know it, as a tourist, and an American one at that, Harry was illegally entering Communist China without a visa—at a time when getting one would have been very difficult, if not impossible. The Cold War was still on. The USSR had not yet fallen, and the U.S. State Department still held Communism as the world's number one problem. But he did say he was bored, right?

Unimpressed by his own bravado, Harry went on.

"Yeah. I just got on it. I was a little bit worried, but I thought as long as that bus stops, and I remember where [the stop] is, I can retrace, you know? So I go about ten miles and I thought that I might as well get off and see what I could see. So I got off and walked down a side road, and there was this big pond there with thousands of ducks … The place was loaded with ducks, walking around or swimming on the water. I wondered, 'What the hell keeps those ducks from flying away?' So I asked a guy. I struck up, you know, a broken English conversation with a Chinese guy walking there. He said, 'They no go. They stay. They born here. I raise them.' That's what he did. He was a duck farmer. We talked some more, and he said he'd kill hundreds at a time. Everybody wanted ducks."

Peking Duck—the very epitome of Chinese cuisine—still on the wing at a free-range duck farm. Harry's storytelling was pretty good, I thought. Exactly how good I had yet to appreciate.

Seeing me smile, Harry continued with practiced nonchalance. "It was interesting, you know? A couple of hours later a bus came along heading back, and I took it and went over to the [water's] edge and took the boat back over to Hong Kong, which is where we were staying."

That was it. Harry stopped and looked pointedly at his watch. The bridge lesson. But I needed a little more for his memoir, something like introspection.

"Well, Harry, what did you take away from your adventure? What did you learn?"

He said he'd heard the Chinese weren't very friendly. "But I figured out that was just a lot of gossip. The Chinese I met, like that duck guy, were very nice people and they had some big jobs. … Everybody says you've got to watch Communist China, but what the hell, you've got to watch everybody. Look, I'm gonna be late here."

As Harry got up, his robe flapped, flashing his underwear. The meeting was over. I sprang up to follow him striding out the door.

"How about next week, same time?" (With Harry, I'd been told, you had to book at least a week in advance. He was that busy.)

"Yeah, sure. Gotta go." He had set the hook well.

And off we both went, he to learn contract bridge, I to ponder the surreality of our first meeting.

As I drove away, my mind tumbled through what I knew about Harry Phelps. *Retired blue-collar worker. World War II vet. Machinist. Watchmaker. Family man with ten children. A guy whose visiting hospice nurse had told me "has some interesting war stories, if you can get him to slow down enough to tell them." AND a guy who'd casually related a tale about entering Communist China, just a few years after the reign of terror of Chairman Mao Zedong, saying he did so more or less because he was just bored one day.* I concluded: *Is this a great writing opportunity, or what?*

I knew Harry was dying, but only because that is what I'd been told. Oh, there had been that oxygen machine in the corner of the room—not even in use. The only other clue to Harry's condition was his wardrobe choice—just robe and slippers every time we met. Moreover, unlike most other residents, that seemed to be all he wore around the Rebecca Residence. I saw him dressed like that in other places: at a card table with others; in a meeting room listening to a presentation; and once in the hallway—on his way back from somewhere to his apartment for our next interview. Scheduled solid. As I said, Harry was a very busy fellow for someone in hospice care.

* * *

In four interviews I would learn a lot more about Harry Phelps. He had a *lot* of stories to tell. One tale genuinely impressed me. It touched on a long personal fascination.

When I was a boy, I collected plastic model airplanes—something like fifty of them. Carefully gluing and painting the models, I stoked my in interest in flying machines. Among these had been the first Wright Flyer, the first jet plane, warplanes, then the rockets that were to orbit the earth and those fictional ones that might take men to the moon one day. Each was prominently positioned on shelves in my bedroom, and each held a special place in my world. I was a youngster growing up through the dawn of the space age. Even today my fascination with machines that fly is still strong.

So imagine my delight when I learned that the busy man I was interviewing had flown in one of the most distinctive planes in my childhood collection —the first of its kind. Harry Phelps told it as simply another story, no more remarkable to him than any of the rest. But I was mesmerized.

Like millions of men of his era, Harry was drafted into the Army in World War II. He came of age toward the end of conflict. Even coming late, like scores of others, Harry contributed to the massive effort that made the Allies victorious in Europe. Of course, on the mundane, everyday scale, an individual's participation rarely seemed so grandiose. And those who have served in the military well know the serviceman's universal motto: "Hurry up and wait." It was not in Harry's character to endure much of that.

Temporarily stationed southwest of Stuttgart when he first arrived, well behind the front lines, Harry found, "We were in there doing nothing much—a little training and cleaning the place up a little bit."

"But Harry, you had to be doing *something*."

"I didn't do anything in the Army," he replied. "My class of work wasn't worth two cents to the Army." That class of work being precision machinist, but my question had launched Harry into another story.

"It was crazy. Every morning they would call out, 'Anybody here a typist?' They asked for a typist four or five days in a row, and I'm getting disgusted because I'm not doing anything. So I tell one of the guys in the room with me, 'The next time he calls for a typist, by God I'm a typist!' He said I was kidding, but I said, 'I am like hell. If that's all they want in this Army, then that's what I'm going to be.' Well, the next morning they asked for another typist, so I put my hand up."

"Harry, didn't they challenge you? Ask what training you had, maybe?"

They did. Harry simply bluffed. "I said, 'You saw me put my hand up, didn't you?' I'd seen a typewriter and I knew I could do it as good as the guy using it."

So Harry was reassigned as a typist and transferred to an engineering company operating and maintaining a considerable number of heavy trucks at a captured Nazi base outside the medieval German town of Fulda. Strange as it might seem, his impatience to be useful positioned him for something else entirely, an absolutely unique life experience, a world-class opportunity. He was to have an adventure only a handful of men on earth had ever had at the time—and those men were elite officers in the German air force.

In 1945, PFC Harry Phelps, a GI from Pittsburgh, got to be one of the fastest men in the world.

Of course, Harry did not claim that. He simply continued his story. "When you're over there on a captured German air base, and there's planes there, and they're just sitting there, you get to wonder who's using 'em. Well, I was delivering some paperwork, so I go and ask and find out that it's our Army Air Corps that moved in there and took over. … Even though the marking on 'em was German.

"So I see a lieutenant coming over, and he asks me what I was doing nosing around, and I said, 'I'm working up in the office, and we're working on the trucks you use every day.' And he says, 'I didn't know that,' and I say, 'Hell no! You're right on top of us and you don't know what we're doing, and we don't know what you're doing!'

"Maybe that got him to think, so he said, 'Well, you come back over here tomorrow, and I'll show you around.' So I said OK."

When Harry went back, he got a tour of not only the base, but also the captured Nazi planes. The lieutenant told Harry (a very easy guy to talk to) that they were flying those German planes, even though they weren't supposed to.

"What else did he tell you that he wasn't supposed to?" I joked.

"Aww, it was just friendship. We were BS-ing a while, and I said I was never up in a plane in my life. And he said, 'Maybe we can get you up in one.' And there was one sitting there."

"It was the first time I ever was even near an airplane in my life … These Messerschmitts were there and they weren't allowed to be flying them, but they were. And when we were climbing up and in, I asked, 'Hey! Where are the propellers?' And he just laughed and said, 'It's a secret.' Then he took me up."

Back on the ground, Harry knew what not to do. "I never told anybody about it before because they didn't want, you know, to get caught … They said, 'Keep it a secret. We could get our tail reamed out for this.' And I said that I knew what they were talking about."

Harry did not appreciate the magnitude of that story. At the time, the aircraft he went up in was the fastest plane in the world.

The Nazis had developed the Messerschmitt 262, the world's first jet-powered ("Where are the propellers?") fighter plane to be deployed by anyone anywhere. Some feel that if the Germans had had that fighter to intercept Allied bombers a year earlier, the ME 262 would have changed the European air war. It was the bane of the U.S. flyers, 100 mph faster than our famous P 51 Mustang's top speed of 500.

After the war, the U.S. forces quickly swept up the captured ME 262s as part of the top-secret "Operation LUSTY" (LUftwaffe Secret TechnologY), as we sought to take advantage of German jet aircraft research and design.

However, by the time Operation LUSTY got to the ME 262s on a captured airfield near Fulda, Harry Phelps had already been there. Opportunist that he was, he'd taken advantage of the situation to cadge a ride on the first operational jet aircraft in history, and to join the elite ranks of the fastest men on the planet.

As an Englishman would say, I was gobsmacked. There I was, sitting with an aging guy dressed in robe and slippers who had flown in the historic German ME 262!

This amazing experience was the result of Harry's reaction to boredom—his fib about being a typist. It was probably a low-risk fib. Being mechanically inclined and the typewriter being essentially, after all, a machine to print words on paper, Harry felt he could master it. And he did. But the opportunity to have this adventure included not only his openness to *find* adventure, but also his realization that there was probably something to be gained by nosing around the captured Nazi air base.

I didn't get to that sort of observation with just these two stories. It was Harry's next even more improbable story that led me to wonder how he did it—how he managed to find and exploit opportunities.

On our third visit, Harry told me a story that started in the more charted waters of his work experience as a machinist. Don't forget that he was doing nothing in the Army related to his craft. He was busy being a motor pool typist. Had he been content to do only that, a unique contribution to the U.S. war effort would not have happened. But Harry saw opportunity everywhere—even in German plumbing.

Harry saw a problem with water. Naturally, the German faucets and plumbing fittings that the U.S. Army encountered were threaded in the metric system. But the hoses and couplings of the Army's water equipment were threaded in the American system. Connecting one to the other was the problem. Harry solved it by designing an adapter that had metric threads on one side and American threads on the other. It was a simple thing with no moving parts. And it could be fabricated on any lathe—including captured German ones.

Harry also realized that the adapter could be used not only at his local base, but also by the Army throughout Europe. So he went to his commanding officer with his drawings and said, "Here's what I'd like to make—an adapter to transfer from metric to our [American] system. Here are the measurements of it—what diameter … inside and outside."

With its lengthy chain of command, the Army was not an easy sell. "Finally I got [my commanding officer] interested in it. He said, 'That sounds good to me, but I'm afraid to ask the colonel up there.' I said, 'What have I got to lose?'

"Now, I don't know the colonel, but I know his first sergeant, who came over with me. I went in there and asked him about his boss. So I said, 'I'll tell you what I want to do. I want to make adapters for the hydrants so we can use them.' I said, 'I got a drawing here. You want to show it to him? But don't tell him where it came from until you get a yes or no.'

"The sergeant didn't grasp the significance. 'It's a good idea, but what's it got to do with the war?'"

With Harry's cajoling, the sergeant showed Harry's design to the colonel anyway. The colonel said, "Who came up with this idea?" and the sergeant told him about Harry out there in the truck company. The colonel OK'd the prototype. It worked, of course.

According to Harry, his design saw widespread adoption in the Army. He had pushed it up the chain of command, and that chain of command was appreciative. "In changing the hydrants from metric to American, we all got a raise. [My commanding officer] did too. He was a second looie [lieutenant] and they made him a first looie."

"Usually an increase in pay means an increase in rank too. What happened, to you, Harry?"

"I was getting to that. I was only a private then and they wanted to make a sergeant out of me—a buck sergeant. That's jumping three grades. But the war was over by then, and then it was 'all fathers go home.' So right then and there I stopped it. There was a fellow I always liked—always treated me good—in our outfit. So I said, 'Give it to him, because he's a good man and he's smart.' He didn't have any children, like me, so he'd be in there four years or so."

"So you gave your promotion to another fellow who was staying in, since as a father you'd be getting out sooner?"

"Yes. And he said, 'You don't have to do this.' I said, 'Hey, somebody's gonna get it. Take it while it's there. Don't argue with me.' So he took it. He used to write me letters from over there once in a while. It was all OK. I'd already gotten my vacation out of it."

"What was that? A vacation?"

I can't have heard him right.

"I was lucky. I had a good CO. He said, 'You take a month and go. You earned it. Get out and see Germany, if you want to.'" The fellow wanted to express his gratitude for Harry's inventiveness.

The war in Europe had just ended. Equipped only with some Army maps, Harry set off alone in his own private jeep to see the country. His parents had spoken German at home, so he'd picked up a little of the language. Even so, he was a stranger to the war-ravaged land. For more than a month Harry toured Germany alone in a jeep by day and stayed overnight in U.S. bases and camps. I had never heard of such a thing—and neither have any of the veterans I've since described Harry's windfall to.

"Harry, exactly how did you manage to get by?"

He started by asking. "In German I'm asking Germans, 'Any U.S. bases around?' Then I'd just go where they said. I'd drive right up and the first thing I'd say: 'Give me some gas. Give me an extra tank.' That was always the first thing.

"At the beginning I was a little bit worried about the jeep at night. But then I figured out that nobody would touch an unattended jeep because they were usually assigned to officers, VIPs. I had orders that said I could go wherever I wanted. That was it. I guess I was a VIP too.

"I went all the way down into Munich. I didn't know where in the hell I was going, either. I got lost many, many, many a time. I'd finally ask somebody who didn't look as though they were afraid of me, to tell me where to go. Then that's where I'd go."

"Just how far did you get?"

"I was getting to that. I went everywhere. I ended up, one time, right on the Swiss border. I thought I'd take a chance and see if I could get in. The Swiss border guard said, 'What are you doing here?' He spoke English to me. I said, 'I'm not doing anything. I'm on vacation. I'd like to go in and see your country.

"He said, 'Would you now?' And he had a backup too—there were two of them there, both with guns. 'You are a U.S. GI. You have a GI jeep with 346th Engineers in the front. And you want to just drive into Switzerland? The only way you'll get in here is over my dead body!'

"He was kind of nasty. 'Now if you get out of that uniform and get out of that Jeep and come back, then I'll let you in.' I was laughing like hell. I said, 'I'm not crazy. I'd like to get in and see your country. The war's over.'"

"He said, 'Maybe, but this craziness will go on for God knows how long till they tell us to pull away. We don't know how long.' I said, 'I understand.' So I never went back."

"What an amazing adventure you had, Harry!"

Harry just brushed it off. "That was on the QT too, you know. Just between me and my CO. When I came back north, just for fun I drove on up to the Kaserne." Panzer Kaserne was headquarters for the German tank corps and a training school for tank crews, I later learned.

"There was a guy up there I thought I'd go to see. He was a GI from Philadelphia who had a truck driver's job in the Army. I'd met him on the boat. When I saw him, I asked, 'How do you like the jeep I got?' He said, 'You son of a bitch! I knew you were gonna be something, but I didn't know you were going to get your own jeep.' I said, 'What the hell are you talking about?' He said, 'I know lieutenants that don't even have their own jeep.' I said, 'Well, that's because of what outfit they're in—what their duties are.' [He said] 'Oh yeah? What're your duties?' I said 'They're pretty big and they're drawn out and take a lot of explaining, and I'm not explaining them to you!'

"So I just took off back to base."

Harry's trip was strictly on a "need to know basis." And no one needed to know he was probably the only GI ever to get a month's vacation to see the sights. I'd made it a point to ask him about that word "vacation." It seems that the whole time he was touring around, he was *not* on leave—he was on active duty. His written orders were simply to go wherever he wanted.

* * *

As I worked on Harry's memoir, it became clear that his life apparently consisted of taking advantage of opportunities that, well, seemed to simply materialize. No grand career plan. No plan for anything, apparently. Just a keen sense of perceiving an opportunity and then acting to take advantage of it.

Like they said in my grandmother's neighborhood, "The dog that trots about finds a bone." To increase your odds of finding a bone of opportunity, you should *actively* look for one. Harry was always on the lookout.

Harry's second secret to enjoying opportunity is probably as obvious as the first: You have to *recognize* an opportunity as such—to be actively receptive to opportunity, all the time. Another old saw says this well: "A threat is merely an opportunity in disguise."

I titled Harry's memoir "Answering Opportunity's Knock." He liked that a lot.

Harry's stories about life after the war were no less astonishing. He turned almost any description into a story.

For instance, Harry had ten children. To feed a dozen mouths, he held down three jobs. The main one was a full-time machinist at a government facility that turned coal into gasoline. He also repaired watches evenings and weekends, and set up voting machines in Allegheny County at election time.

"Harry, did you ever do anything but work?"

"Well, you do what you gotta do. The watch work I did at home. I outfitted a workbench in my basement. And the voting machine work I got into right at the end of the war.

"We got about $5 an hour when I started. And after more than fifteen years, they wouldn't give us a raise. You didn't know whether to ask for one or not. I asked some of the other guys, 'Do you think we ought to be working for this kind of money? Why can't we get a raise?' We were listed as machinists, you know. Finally the one guy and me, we got the bosses stirred up a little bit. We asked [the] good guy who ran the whole shop. And he said, 'Yeah. You guys deserve more money. I've been thinking that for a couple of years. But you weren't making any noise, so I thought you were satisfied. Now I'll go and ask the big shots [for a dollar an hour more].'"

If you never even ask the question, the answer is already "no."

"Anyway, we got the raise without any trouble at all."

"Since we are talking about money, Harry, how did you ever entertain ten children? And how about vacations?"

Harry chuckled and launched into another story.

"I took ten kids and a wife in a CarryAll," a forerunner to GM's giant Suburban SUV. "I bought an Army surplus tent and we all had sleeping bags. We learned to go camping. We started not far from Pittsburgh—thirty miles south—Raccoon State Park. It was a big park, and it was beautiful. Then the first night I heard some rattling. The raccoons were trying to get into my potatoes. I didn't think [to put] them up in a tree. And they got ahold of them and it didn't take 'em long to eat them all. So I learned to keep the damn potatoes and all of the rest of the food up in the trees away from the 'coons. There were so many of them. One night I went out with my flashlight—all I could see were eyes! Where the hell did they all come from?

"So after that excitement, we went camping every year. But we did it before it was the rage and we did it on the cheap. Later, people had fancy trailers with crank-out awnings so they could sit outside like kings, you know. And I said, 'You people with money can do that—I can't.' That camping was the only way I could figure out how to afford a vacation for everybody."

"Sounds like you came up with a way to have a vacation every year. But was there anything you did for fun, for recreation from work, the rest of the year?"

"I really liked to ice skate," he said. "I've always done it. I had a beautiful pair of figure skates that I used for years."

He was about 12 when he started. "I skated any place I could. When I was young, we even froze a skating rink at Olympia Park. It was right down from my house, down Grandview Avenue." The boys in the neighborhood would make a rink out of packed snow, fill it with water, and let it freeze overnight.

"When I was a kid, I skated all day long. I wouldn't even come home for dinner. I was over there from two in the afternoon to seven at night. I'd stay out there 'cause if the ice was perfect, there's nothing like figure skating.

"And that reminds me about skating in Washington."

"Washington … Did you go there just to skate, Harry?"

Might as well take the bait.

"I don't know what in the hell I was in DC for. It was back when I was in the Army, and it was the middle of winter, I know that. Well, I saw that big lake, right off of the [Washington] Monument. It's a long body of water. And it was frozen solid."

"Harry, I think that had to be the famous Lincoln Memorial Reflecting Pool that runs from the Washington Monument to the Lincoln Memorial—it's more than a third of a mile long!"

"Well, whatever it was, I thought, 'What the hell. There's nobody skating on that.' So I called my wife back home and said, 'How about sending my skates out here?' She said, 'What are you going to do?' I said, 'I'm gonna skate on this Reflection whatever they call it.' She sent them and I got out there after I ate breakfast one morning. And I'm skating.

"First thing you know, there's a couple cars pull up. It was the police and they weren't happy.

"You'd think I was Al Capone or somebody. They were blowing their whistles and yelling at me and all. They took me in. They took my name and fingerprinted me and everything else. I said, 'What the hell are you doing? I'm in the Army.' They said, 'So what? You're trespassing on government property.'

"They gave me the third degree—two hours, I'll bet. Then, finally, they said, 'Don't come back. Ever.' And I said, 'Don't worry, I don't ever want to fool with you any more.'

"But it had been beautiful! Man, I'd skated all around! All the way up and back. But since I was the only one out there, I thought to myself, 'I bet I'm not supposed to be here.' I knew that, you know, but what the hell. Ha! When those cars pulled up, I knew what I was in for."

Perhaps many had looked longingly at the inviting ice that winter, but only Harry Phelps had the nerve to test it. He saw an opportunity and took advantage of it. Even though something didn't look quite right, why not give it a try? Opportunity knocks just once, you know. So maybe Harry Phelps was, perhaps will forever be, the only person ever to ice skate on the famed Lincoln Memorial Reflecting Pool.

* * *

Though he had told many a well-practiced story, most with a touch of humor, Harry Phelps had not been a guy to bond with. He was simply too busy. Although prompt for our interviews and trusting me to finish on time, he always had something else to get to. In a managed care facility, slowing down is expected. That just wasn't Harry Phelps.

The February afternoon I turned over the final copies of his memoir, Harry thanked me warmly and sincerely. He said one of his daughters had read the draft and now all of his many children were asking when they would get to read it too. In his robe and slippers, Harry was seated in an easy chair in his and Helen's living room. For the first time I saw him using the oxygen machine that had been there all the while.

I hadn't formally scheduled an appointment; I just called and drove over. We talked a little about what it had been like to work together. I thanked him for telling his stories and repeated that he'd never given me much insight into how he'd felt about the amazing things he had done. We'd talked about this before. And as before, Harry just shrugged.

Then, right on the hour, he once more made a show of looking at his watch.

"I'm sorry. I gotta go upstairs to the activity room. I heard a couple guys when I was passing the dining room yesterday talking about being bored, and now we're thinking about maybe starting a chess club or something."

Then, with an uncharacteristic flicker of reflection, "You know, my hospice nurse said maybe I should slow down."

But instantly the pragmatic Harry returned. "So I asked her, and she told me maybe she could get me a portable oxygen setup. Carry it with a shoulder strap."

Once more a pause as Harry turned to study the stark winter trees outside the window.

Pensive?

I waited for Harry to break the silence, and, of course, he did. "I'm wondering how it works. There's no tank, so it must take it out of the air or something. Wonder if I can figure out how it works? Maybe I'll try to open it up."

Classic Harry. Just another opportunity.

Journey: Finding Hospice

I visited both inpatient hospice facilities the hospital social worker had told me about. And I was amazed.

I was expecting an environment something like a hospital or a nursing home. Brightly lit utilitarian hallways flanked by semi-private patient rooms. Wheelchairs and medical carts of various function in the halls, some busily attended by workers. Shiny, hard, easy-to-clean surfaces everywhere. A whiff of antiseptic in the air, pervaded by the din of constant activity all around. All five of the hospitals and the nursing home I'd had Frank in were like that.

But neither hospice was like that. Instead, the ambiance was a lot like a private home. A normal residential door opened onto what looked like—actually was—a living room. Further along, there was a nurses' station, but without the continual bustle. Even the hallways were somehow softer, not at all like a hospital but more like a hotel, except wider, better lit and with some attention to décor. And the patient rooms, all single occupancy, looked just like bedrooms in a home: There was wooden furniture—a dresser and a TV stand instead of an overhead suspension. There wasn't any gleaming imposing wall escutcheon with oxygen, and vacuum, and electric and who knows what other connections. No ceiling suspensions to hang IV bottles.

And the differences extended beyond the patient facilities to those for visitors as well. Instead of glaringly bright hospital "waiting areas" for anxious relatives, with institutional chairs and old, tatty magazines in a heap next to a blaring TV, each hospice had what resembled a living room, with comfortable, upholstered chairs and wooden end and coffee tables. And they had incandescent lamps instead of harsh overhead fluorescents. Everywhere there was actual décor: peaceful paintings and floral arrangements. Nothing sumptuous—just the ambiance of a middle-class home. This was how it was at both in-patient hospices I visited.

And as for TVs, whose glaring screens and chortling audio seem to be everywhere, there were none anywhere, except in patient rooms. No background of hawking din. No attention high-jacking imagery.

Most of all, in stark contrast to the continuous cacophony of hospital and nursing home, it was peaceful. It was serene. It was calming.

All this was no accident. This soothing, familiar ambiance was obviously planned.

One of the hospices also had a kitchen with a sink, a range, and a refrigerator—just like any other home. Even though I was told that patients' meals were prepared elsewhere in the facility, it was a real kitchen, with a fruit bowl on the table. And the people sitting at that table, clearly the relatives or friends of a patient, were having a quiet conversation like those at any kitchen table. Sitting there having doughnuts, the smell of fresh coffee on the air.

It was difficult to imagine that a healthcare facility could be less like a healthcare facility than those hospices were.

There was much of the same equipment as in a hospital, like medicine carts and oxygen, but all that was kept out of sight unless in use. There were never unattended carts parked in the hall. The feeling was that of a home, maybe not your own, but *someone's* home. Warm and familiar, not artificial. Not harsh. There were even personal touches, knick-knacks and found art.

My mind said: "People are living here." And of course, they—the patients—were.

I talked to the RN hospice supervisor at both facilities. They came out and sat with me in the living rooms. They explained it to me.

I especially remember talking to Diana Meade, the supervising nurse at the inpatient hospice unit at Concordia in Cabot, Pennsylvania. In particular I asked a lot about medications and what the procedures were for administering them. Diana told me that hospices have standing orders from the hospice doctors that give more flexibility to the nurse on duty to make judgments on what and how much medication is needed. They make these judgments on the spot. Only in unforeseen circumstance does a doctor even need to be consulted.

She gently let me know that they had a lot of experience with people who are dying—that is the only kind of patient they have.

I thought about all the nurses in the hospital who had reacted so differently to my requests for more medication, and I thought about the ones who would then search for a doctor in the hospital to get approval, all while my uncle suffered and I anxiously paced.

Diana told me how patients are "looked in on" every hour to see if they are in any sort of discomfort, but are otherwise undisturbed, except for hygiene tasks.

I thought about nurses taking Frank's vitals throughout day and night and painfully turning him unnecessarily.

She told me how meals might be comforting sometimes and how, depending on the patient's closeness to death and their personal wish, they might or might not be wanted, and that the staff would comply with each individual.

I thought of dozens of meals coming to Frank's room, only to be cleared away uneaten, and I thought about Good-With-Patients Bob practically force-feeding Frank his breakfast.

Diana wanted to know about Frank—not his medical condition, but who he was and what he liked. And I told her how he'd lived alone and the vow I'd made in the hospital that he not die alone. I told her that as in the hospital, I'd be staying nights.

Diana took my hand in hers, "You know, I've been a hospice nurse for a long time, and I know how you feel. Just let me say that I've seen a lot of people and their families struggle with this, and we will support you with whatever you decide. But from my experience I've found that if a patient is supposed to be alone when they depart, that's the way it will be. And if they are supposed to be with family, it will be that way. I guess what I'm saying is Providence will decide, and it will be all right."

That was enough.

Right there, I decided.

And that was one of the best—and by best, I mean "most correct"—decisions of my life. The Good Samaritan Hospice was the right place for Frank.

With all the suffering and anguish we had been through in the last two weeks, if ever anyone was in need of a good Samaritan, it was Frank and I.

Driving back immediately from the hospice in Cabot, I initiated Frank's discharge from the hospital that afternoon. It was supposed to happen first thing the next morning. It coincided with the last day of his hospital medical coverage. Nevertheless, it literally took the entire working day—eight hours—for them to get Frank out of the hospital and into an ambulance for the ride to Cabot. He slept most of the day. And they thoughtfully gave him pain medication in advance of moving him into the ambulance. As it pulled out of the hospital bay, those of us who had come to accompany Frank to the hospice formed a caravan of cars behind it for the drive north.

Frank was still asleep when we arrived at the hospice around dinnertime.

The Inpatient Unit of the Good Samaritan Hospice is at the Concordia Lutheran Ministries senior living center on Marwood Road in Cabot, Pennsylvania—"The Unit," as it is called—has just eleven beds. When he arrived, Frank was one of only three patients in the facility. In light of the tens of thousands of people who were in that hospice's territory, obviously it was clear that I was not the only one who had never heard about hospice in general or The Unit in particular.

As Frank, still asleep, was eased into his bedroom-like setting, night descended. The others who had come from the hospital had departed, but I asked to stay. Still wary from the trauma of the hospital, I was apprehensive about leaving Frank alone.

Later, as I dozed off, I began to truly believe that things actually might be different here. Frank's medications were being administered as needed and without delay. They told me that morphine could be given under the tongue, injected, in pill, or in patch form. Diana had told me that each of these "modalities" had different profiles of pain release over time. In the hospital there had been only injection. It seemed that the hospice personnel knew more about this particular medication than the people at the hospital. And that makes sense. In a hospital, morphine is seen as a last resort, so use of it is avoided due to fear of addiction. And since it is therefore not used as often, its various effects are neither so crucial to understand nor experienced nearly as often as in a hospice.

Frank did get oxygen, as well, though not from an ominous multifunction wall escutcheon. A portable oxygen machine was set up next to his bed. "Really, with lung function problems, it's important. Without enough oxygen, no matter what else is going on, you would feel like you were drowning without it," Diana had said. It wouldn't make him better, just more comfortable.

At The Unit, even though I spent the night on a couch with pillow and blanket, I slept much more soundly than in the never-darkened, always noisy hospital. Frank was sleeping too—plainly less agitated. When they came hourly to "look in" on Frank, neither of us was awakened.

Satisfied that Frank was in good hands, I left the hospice in the morning and drove the many miles home to have a shower and some breakfast. I'd talked to the nurses before leaving. They felt that Frank was not likely to awaken. It seemed they knew the stages that one goes through as the end draws near, so I asked, and they gave me a pamphlet entitled *Gone From My Sight,* which describes how people look and behave in different stages as life ebbs. The nurses felt it would be no more than a day or two at most for Frank.

I returned late in the afternoon. I was satisfied that I no longer had to rush and hover over Frank just to insure his care was appropriate. I was able to breathe a little easier.

That evening my cousin, Frank's niece, Cindy Wargo and her husband, John, made the trip to Cabot to see Frank. Of course all of his nephews and nieces who could make it had come to see him back in the hospital. As a matter of fact that had caused me some uneasiness, since I didn't know what Frank would have wanted in terms of visitors and their behavior.

But at the hospice, Cindy and I went in to Frank's room together and just sat in silence with him for a while. He was at peace, breathing slowly, shallowly, but without labor, the oxygen hissing into him through a nose cup. I got up and left, giving Cindy some time alone with him. I'd already said everything to Uncle Frank that I had to say on our many long nights together at the hospital. We'd had some interesting discussions in his lucid moments. For instance, one night when were both awake, I'd asked him what he'd been looking for in spending so much time at the library before his ankle incident. Frank simply answered, "The truth." And that began a philosophical discussion that ended at dawn with the day's first obligatory taking of vitals and painful turning of Frank.

Leaving Cindy, I went out on the front porch of The Unit into the warm summer night. In a few minutes Cindy came out dabbing her tears. We sat silently in the humid air alive with the chirping of crickets and rasps of katydids.

We had not seen each other in years, so we started to talk. Of course we spoke about Frank mostly. Cindy had spent the first part of her childhood with Frank and his father who lived in the apartment above her parents' place. She knew a lot more about his habits than I did. Yet it seems that as far as family was concerned, he had always preferred to keep to himself, even though his sister and her family of five lived just one floor below. Cindy and I talked more, moving on to our own lives and what had happened to us since we last had met.

We were still reminiscing at a few minutes to ten o'clock on that humid August night when the hospice nurse on duty opened the door and said, "I think you'd better come inside." We'd been out on the porch for little more than an hour.

Once we were in the living room of The Unit, the nurse simply said, "Frank just died. We were doing our check when we discovered this. I'm sorry. Please go to see him."

Frank had died alone.

I remembered Diana Meade's words when I'd first talked with her: "If Providence means for them to die alone, then that's the way it will be."

Images of the last two weeks when I spent every night with Frank at the hospital flashed by. But now, here at the hospice, I realized that although I'd vowed to be with Frank when he died, I'd never thought to ask him about it. Like most people, I was just too afraid or ashamed to speak openly *to him* about his dying. Certainly, death was always the elephant in the room, but to mention its name was unthinkable—even to someone who had made the conscious decision to live no longer.

I'd been a constant advocate for Frank, and back in the hospital he'd certainly needed one. But here at the hospice unit—for the first time in the exclusive care of people interested only in making him comfortable—Frank and I both had a chance to relax. And I like to think that when Frank at last relaxed, he no longer resisted the unknown. He simply, peacefully, let it claim him.

Although the time of a death is solemn, we only can know about that time through the experience of the living.

Cindy and I stayed with Frank for a few more minutes. I don't know what was on her mind, but on mine, there was only the thought of loss. My loss. And for what might have been for Frank. My tears came naturally.

After a time, as we sat next to the bed in the darkened bedroom where Frank lay, something edged in on our private thoughts. Although it was nearing midnight, there came down the hallway an unmistakable aroma. The sweetly comforting scent of something in an oven.

It was almost midnight, and someone was baking.

Roused from our personal reveries so considerately, Cindy and I went out from Frank's darkened room into the hall and down toward the snug kitchen next to the living room.

There, in the midst of death—Frank's death—we shared an affirmation of life, our lives. It was a simple thing, fresh, hot cookies and coffee.

Food is for the living—those left behind. How the hospice staff knew to make such a connection, I can't fathom. But it typifies the sort of thing that would never happen—could never happen—in a hospital. The hospice nurse sat with us at a homey kitchen table and had a cookie and a little coffee too, as she quietly listened and talked about a man whom she had only known for a day. She spoke about what she could, the peacefulness of his departure over the last thirty hours. That was how long Frank had been at The Unit.

I could have brought him here two weeks ago. Why hadn't I?

At last, just after midnight, Cindy and I hugged our goodbyes. We had silently agreed to wait together until the coroner's van had come for Frank. Now there was nothing more to do but go home.

Frank's book of life had closed. And a new chapter was opening in mine.

I knew I'd have to do something to redress the way things had gone for Frank and me. But first, I would have to finish up my responsibilities to the man who had wanted to be alone.

As he wished, Frank was cremated. There was no viewing. There was no service of any kind. His ashes were to be consigned to his place in the family plot in Allegheny Cemetery near where he had lived most of his life. All this was in accordance with what he had laid out in his will. Responsible as his named executor, I saw to it that his wishes were met. Some in the family had wanted to do otherwise, but they were not the one who Frank chose.

And so it was alone that I executed all of the necessary documents, saw to his cremation, dealt with the cemetery and procured a marker for his grave. And, preceded by no memorial service of any kind, it was alone that I went to witness Frank's interment.

The workmen opened the grave and by law had to put in a small concrete vault sized to contain Frank's ashes. On a sunny September day I looked on as they sealed the little vault and filled the small hole with earth. I gave each of the three of them a twenty—not a tip, really, just a thank you to three working men from another, Frank Piasecky.

The plain marker that the VA provided gratis for veterans would be installed later. Frank had wanted only that, that small, flush, bronze plaque. So after a few minutes of looking out from his hilltop grave toward the residential cityscape of the Pittsburgh neighborhood of Lawrenceville, a scene Frank had been part of for most of his life, I turned and left his resting place and the cemetery itself.

I dodged across busy Butler Street. It was late morning and rush-hour traffic had been replaced by the day's normal procession of vehicles down Lawrenceville's main artery.

Before going into the diner across the street, I decided to try the door to the tavern next door. The place was open. I sat down at the bar. I ordered two shots of Jack Daniel's—one for me and one for Frank. I lifted my own shot to my lips and stared at the other. No toast. No memorial. My only thought was how fitting it was to do this in the morning, which was the time of day when Frank and I might once have done this together. While he was working, visitors always came in the morning—after his night shift and before he went to bed.

I thought back over the last few weeks, trying to sort out what had made everything so difficult. Most painful were the memories of Frank in the hospital, when he couldn't tell me what he wanted, and I had to guess. I remembered *The Five Wishes*[*] booklet I had learned about at the hospice. If I'd only known of Frank's wishes, things would have been much easier for me, and for Frank, too.

 Most people are aware of three of The Five Wishes: a will (a legal document), to describe what you wish to happen with your assets and possessions once you are gone; a Living Will (another legal document), to tell what you want in the way of medical care in the case that you cannot say so yourself; and a Healthcare Power of Attorney (a third formal document), to designate someone to act legally on your behalf should you become incapacitated.

However, it is the last two wishes that make the Five Wishes booklet so valuable. The fourth one is where you to indicate how you wish to be treated should you not be able to say so—a place for you to put it in black and white. And the fifth one is for you to state how you want to be remembered.

Frank had that, the fifth wish, in his will—absolutely no remembrance of any sort, except for the VA-provided grave marker. But as to the fourth wish, I had no way to know how he wanted to be treated by others when he was incapacitated. So I'd had to guess. Not knowing Frank's wishes, at one point I acquiesced to others and let them crowd into his hospital room, hug him and kiss him. Someone turned on the TV, which Frank had never asked to be done in his last two weeks. Incongruously, they tuned in a baseball game. All the while I worried whether any of this was what a man who'd always chosen to be alone would want. And the talk and conversation in the room—it was as though the man in the hospital bed was not there at all, much less to die shortly. Looking back, I know it was my responsibility to control this situation, and I hadn't. If only I had known Frank's wishes.

As I sat in the bar late in the morning, I decided that I would purchase and mail copies of the Five Wishes booklet directly to all my friends and relatives. I wanted to try to spare as many of them

[*] The Five Wishes booklet is available online and can be found at https://agingwithdignity.org

as I could from the doubt I'd had to endure in not knowing what Frank would have wanted. There: something I could *do*.

As my shot of Jack Daniel's warmed my empty stomach and I looked on at Frank's, I thought again about hospice, too. I'd had to learn about the booklet the same way I'd had to learn about hospice—the hard way—when faced with an emergency situation and having no time at all to think. But mostly I was aware of Frank's extra suffering in the hospital due to my personal ignorance. I could have gotten him to hospice a week earlier. That really bothered me. I knew I must find a way to help others— anyone who would listen—to realize they should look into hospice care *now*, before they, too, must face the same situations I had. I knew I needed to actually *do* something about that. Otherwise Frank's suffering, and mine, too, would have been in vain.

With a whispered "*Na zdrovie*, Frank," the traditional Old Country toast, I downed his shot in Frank's name. I hoped he would forgive that modicum of remembrance. The toast was one we'd made to each other many times before.

I laid a twenty on the bar and made my way next door to breakfast.

* * *

I'd been profoundly affected—changed, really—by our hospice experience. The people I met there were all so different from the medical people I had been in contact with throughout my life. For one thing, they all seemed to be more serene. And they all were more caring—about Frank to be sure, but also about me. I came to understand that hospice is as much for the survivors as it is for the patient. They know that losing someone close is one of life's greatest stressors. And they strive to make it as easy and as peaceful as they can for you to deal with what you must deal with. While medical personnel in doctors' offices and hospitals work to keep their ambiance clinical and businesslike, hospice professionals try to make theirs warm and human.

I have come to characterize hospice nurses and aids this way: While you are still on this earth, they are as close as you can come to knowing saints.

Before my personal experience with Frank's death, I would have written off such a thought as sentimental hyperbole. Now, I don't think it is. Every day that hospice workers go to work they deal with death, frequently of people they have gotten to know. Every day they are graphically aware of the mortality of us all, including themselves. Every day they help with the pain of loss that death brings to those left behind, and more to the point, at the very moment it is at its height.

It would be absurd to think that their many experiences do not mold hospice personnel in some way. And I think that the way that it does so is to make them the most sensitive, caring people you will ever meet in the healthcare field, or any other, for that matter.

Hospice people *know* how precious, yet how ephemeral, life is.

They see it taken from people every day. They see what loss that creates every day. And in seeing so much of it they know more certainly than the rest of us, whom our culture carefully insulates from death and dying, the true value of life. They respect and cherish life as few others consciously do. And they know that the only antidote for grief is love—freely and unconditionally given in the brief time we all have to give it. They give it to the dying and to the living in equal measure. Like saints surely do, they know what is really important, *every* day.

Even years later, knowing what I had cost Frank by not immediately getting him into hospice deeply troubles me. And it always will.

Frank could have spent his last two weeks in a loving and tranquil environment instead of the clamorous sterility of the hospital.

I do not shy away from the reason that he did not earlier get the benefit of hospice: It was my ignorance. No matter who else did what they did at Frank's end, I was responsible for his well-being. He was relying on me. And in not knowing about and considering hospice until someone worried about Frank's hospital bill finally decided to tell me it was an option, I had failed him. It had been my responsibility to know.

Of course I'd heard the word, but because I had no notion of what happened in hospice care, I had not thought about it when I should have—when Frank first needed it—when he was first pronounced to be dying.

The thing that kept nagging at me after Frank's ordeal was that we both had paid such a high price, seemingly for nothing. It was in the recognition of the sheer wastefulness of Frank's suffering that I vowed that I must do something, anything, to wrest some value out of our nightmare.

So I set out to try to help others who otherwise could face the same situation. I knew they would need two things that I'd had a shortage of: knowledge of the hospice option and the courage to act upon it. I realized there was little I could do about the latter, but I certainly could find a way to help address the former.

A Writing Partner's Tale: *Courage*

The only real prison is fear,
and the only real freedom is freedom from fear.
Aung San Suu Kyi

The first time I saw Michael Chapman's hands, he was lying in his coffin. They were soft and slender, with trimmed nails and long, expressive fingers—the hands of a pianist, maybe. From his stories about pulling tree stumps, felling timber and clearing boulders, I had pictured the hands of a workman, gnarled and callused, perhaps with a patina of permanently ground-in dirt.

But Michael hadn't used his hands in years, and that's what I was seeing: hands long ago idled by ALS.

Amyotrophic lateral sclerosis, or Lou Gehrig's disease, is fatal. There is no known cure. Slowly your muscles waste away, starting in your extremities and progressing inexorably to your core. Michael was near the end of that progression when we met. His esophagus had begun to atrophy, making swallowing problematic. First, heavy food had had to go—meat and fresh vegetables. Then softer foods—mashed potatoes and purees. That left liquids. But he'd had a severe choking spell anyway. It was a sip of juice that did him in.

Even though he'd been in home hospice care for more than a month, the family had panicked and rushed him to a hospital instead of calling his hospice nurse. Once at the hospital, a place for getting people well again, the family realized their mistake. Michael would never get well again. Regretting their error, his family hurriedly transferred Michael to the hospice inpatient unit where, unresponsive, but at least now comfortable and in a serene place, he spent his last days.

As we'd worked on his memoir, Michael's stories had mostly been from better times, alive with the fresh breeze and warm sunshine of the outdoors. His stories were often about what some would call work—carpentry, clearing land, gardening, fixing and repairing. He had not been one to spend time on music or art. Though he had a master's degree, he was "not a reader." Michael's preferred diversions took him into the fields and woods.

Michael had been a high school teacher for thirty years before he retired. In the summer, he would do the lesson planning for the next year astride his tractor. He said the monotony of the work complemented the intricacies of the planning. In my own career, I'd done an awful lot of plans for products and technologies, but I'd always had to isolate myself at a desk, using paper and pencil to keep track of my thoughts. He'd do it all in his head, then later write out each lesson plan from memory.

Given all of this, it is tempting to picture Michael Chapman as a hale, strapping fellow. However, when I first encountered him he was anything but. He was the most visibly afflicted partner I've ever written with.

Michael and Ellen Chapman's home was set deep in the woodlands of Western Pennsylvania.

Michael's visiting nurse from the Good Samaritan Hospice knew the way. She assured me that GPS and directions were no use in getting to the house. She wisely suggested that we meet at a gas station off the main highway and that I follow her. The description "off the beaten path" was never truer, she said. She was right—I would not have found it on my own. When I got there, the GPS knew where I was, of course, but it did not show me on a road. My car's icon pulsed in the middle of nowhere.

I'd followed the nurse's SUV over roads progressively more and more rural for the last ten of my fifty-mile trip. We ended up miles beyond pavement at a long gravel lane that could barely pass our vehicles through the trees. At its end the track opened out into an expansive, lush meadow rising away from the Chapmans' house nestled at the foot of the park-like field. Michael made the meadow himself. He had cleared several acres out of a rugged, forested slope—one tree and one boulder at a time.

We parked our vehicles on the verge, and I followed the nurse up onto the porch. There, we were loudly greeted by a German shepherd whom I would learn was appropriately named Gabby.

Ellen, Michael's wife, came out to greet us. She was pleasant and petite, with short brown hair and a warm, sincere smile. She bustled us into the house, through the kitchen and toward what had been the living room. Now it was Michael's room, dominated by his hospital bed and the full-length special reclining chair on which he lay.

The wall-to-wall carpeting had been taken up, exposing the plywood subfloor, at odds with the orderly, neat furnishings. I was certain the carpeting had been removed in order to accommodate the various equipment that Michael now needed, like the elaborate motorized wheelchair parked in the kitchen and the person-hoist standing next to it.

On his special recliner, Michael was almost, but not quite, horizontal, facing away from the doorway, almost completely concealed beneath a Pittsburgh Steeler-crested blanket tucked from chin to toe. Only his face was exposed. The weather was not very cold, perhaps in the high 70s, yet on this and all my following visits, Michael was always covered this way, and always with his head turned at exactly the same angle to the same side, propped up with a pillow and a block of foam rubber. Michael's neck was frozen in that position.

Before I could say a word, Michael spoke. Facing as he was, he could not see me, but having heard us come in he said, obviously to me, "Please excuse me for not getting up to shake hands." His voice breathy, nearly inaudible, yet unmistakably wry.

I was not prepared for such a greeting. I mumbled something, but I can't recall what. It wasn't important anyway. What was important was how Michael had chosen to greet me. To defuse what he thought might be an awkward moment, he had made a joke about his condition—about the disease that was inexorably taking his life.

* * *

From the hospice's background information, I knew that Michael Chapman was clear and lucid, and reticent about working on a memoir. His caregivers reported that he simply did not think he had anything interesting to say. I have heard this frequently at the outset of memoir projects. Many people do not think they have done, or been, or experienced, or thought anything that would interest others. By the time we part, this initial worry is replaced by a feeling of accomplishment—sometimes outright elation. I had learned in doing patient memoirs that everybody has something uniquely interesting to say. And when my writing partner sees the story written out in black and white, they usually come to understand it as such, too. I am glad Michael had reconsidered and let me come to work with him. His story was to be as much a learning experience for me as it was an uplifting ideal for others.

That's because with Michael Chapman, I found the most compelling, or perhaps even the most defining, thing framing his stories was the disease that was killing him.

Usually the memoir I jointly produce with a hospice patient is about everything *but* their fatal condition. With Michael Chapman, though, the nature and length of his coping with ALS showed not only the horrors that come with that affliction but also Michael's remarkable way of coping with it.

* * *

It is very difficult for someone who has never experienced it, either personally or through others held close, to fully comprehend the devastation of ALS. That's because it is rare. Annually in the United States, there are only two cases of ALS diagnosed per 100,000 population, which is only 0.02%. Meanwhile the top cause, heart disease, claims 23.4% of all deaths. ALS is way, way down the list. So the notoriety the disease gets is not due to how many men and women it kills each year, but the frightfulness of how it does it.

When I worked with Michael Chapman, he had had ALS for more than five years, already on the high side of the survival rate. After my first interview, I noticed that I felt a kind of apprehension or anticipation when I was with him. I believe that was my unintentional reaction to a person who is totally paralyzed. Something was missing. He made none of the slight movements— the shifts, scratches and finger fidgets—that our subconscious expects of others. At his stage of the disease, Michael could move nothing but his face.

Before going into the other stories Michael told me, let me tell one he made me a part of.

Everyone must pee. This is true for ALS patients too, of course. However, for ALS patients, the very act of urination has to change as hands, then arms become useless. This might seem to be a little off-putting, but I relate it here because it is important to understanding Michael's stories.

Good Samaritan Hospice in-home assistance offers Respite Care, giving family caregivers a chance to take a breather while the patient is cared for in an inpatient hospice unit. Twice I interviewed Michael during a respite stay. On the second visit, after we had been talking for more than an hour and a half, Michael made an odd request.

"How would you like to be number forty-one?"

"I'm sorry, Michael. I didn't quite get that."

"Would you like to be number forty-one to hold the pee bottle for me? I need to use it now."

"Forty-one … You mean …"

"Yep. I've been keeping count. Forty people have had to help me urinate so far. So unless you want to be number forty-one, you'd better go get a nurse."

I guffawed, then sputtered: "You know, Michael, I don't think I'm qualified! I'll go get a nurse. See you next week."

Just like a former math teacher to do such a thing. Chuckling all the way to the nurses' station, I decided to play along.

"Excuse me, but Michael Chapman is asking for number forty-one."

All three nurses burst into laughter, even as one immediately got up to attend to Michael's needs. It seems that his tally was a standing joke.

"He keeps track," a nurse said. "He says it's good for his memory, so we started keeping track too. He has never counted anyone twice. We need to cheat, though. We need to use paper. He keeps it all in his head."

I thought about this as I drove away. There were two things about Michael's tallying. Most obvious was his self-deprecating sense of humor. Making himself the butt of a joke did not bother him at all. I'd realized that from our first meeting. To him, his losses were simply an obvious thing to joke about. Moreover, it seemed to me the power he exercised in keeping track of his bottle holders really put the dependence caused by his disease in its place. And that place was one of triviality—a place for life's little jokes. I realized that he did this for the benefit of both himself and those on whom he had to depend. He pre-empted pity.

In contrast to his complete dependence now, *independence* had been the running theme of most of the stories that Michael had told me—up to the point where he contracted ALS. But then, slowly, persistently, the disease had forced him to become completely dependent on others. And *completely* meant even to the point of needing someone to blot his tears for him as we worked on his memoir. I'd never had to do that for anyone in my life.

That Michael could experience such a total psychic reversal and still maintain a sense of humor about it lay at the heart of his attitude toward the disease.

I made it the central theme in his memoir.

By far, Michael Chapman told me more stories about his tenure as a high school math teacher than any other single topic. Although it had been more than twenty years since they had happened, he remembered them clearly and told them in detail.

"Michael, what do you mean when you say you 'kept to yourself'?"

"Back then, I was kind of known as 'The Invisible Man' because I didn't attend very many social things that the other teachers did. I spent most of my time either in the math office or somewhere alone. I didn't socialize much."

This resonated with me. The feeling of being alone in crowds had led me to avoid them. How had *he* coped?

"Did the other teachers ride you a lot about that?"

"No, not too much. We teachers in the math department seemed to keep to ourselves and not mingle with the other department teachers. We just didn't do much of that. Of course, I'd go down into the teacher's lunchroom once in a while."

Michael was a loner away from work as well. But he was not a recluse. He had a lot to do, taking care of his aging parents and both their house and his property.

"My dad just had an attack one morning and he was gone by evening. But then I had to take care of my mom. I moved her into a house I bought in Ohioville, Pennsylvania. I did that from the time my dad died until her death. She was a sickly person and she was 85 when she passed. I was fortunate. I didn't have to lift her. But she spent most of her time in bed.

"It was pretty hard. I just felt it was my duty, so I did it."

That sense of responsibility would underpin a lot Michael's stories.

Surprisingly, at his retirement at 53, Michael was still a bachelor. And after he retired, he lived alone in his country house for more than a decade, improving the building and working on the grounds—clearing woods and rocks, making what amounts to a rural western Pennsylvania park.

I knew that Michael was married now, so he wasn't really a recluse, like my Uncle Frank had been.

"How come you stayed single so long, Michael?"

"At first I'd kind of felt it was my duty to see my elderly parents through the rest of their life. And then the place in Kittanning, I inherited that property, so for a few years I tried to get it livable—put the new house up and worked on the land.

"And then I just felt it was time for me to meet somebody."

"All of a sudden, after being a bachelor for sixty years?"

"Well, at that point I started going to church. I'd not been a church person up until then. Ellen and I got introduced there—and we started to date and that went on for four years. I met her through a mutual acquaintance."

That was a little too pragmatic. I pried.

"How about telling me what your first date was like."

"I thought she'd be more comfortable if she drove on her own, and if she decided she didn't like me, she could just leave. We went to a restaurant that was halfway between her place and mine. We went in and they had a big menu and we picked our meals out and we had a good dinner there. I picked up the tab. And things went fine."

Seated across the room, Ellen Chapman filled in details from her point of view.

"I kept wondering, 'Why won't he take me to his house?' He'd been to my house enough, but he just kept saying, 'Not yet.' And he also said, 'I will. I need to clean it up.' But that wasn't the real reason."

Michael tried to explain.

"Well, finally I did it and we were going through the back roads to get up here, all forest and trees. And finally we got to my lane, and we started up the lane, and I said, 'Now it's a little ways up here' and we kept going up."

Ellen interposed, "I kept saying, 'Where's the house? Where's the house?' That was why he'd put it off. He was afraid that if he'd told me exactly how far out he lived—and no neighbors—that he'd scare me away. But I wasn't scared at all! I thought that was all pretty cute."

Michael and Ellen courted for more than three years. Michael asked for her hand several times, but having suffered one wrenching marriage, Ellen was cautious. Michael was patient. When Ellen's stepmother told her, "You won't find anybody else as good as him," she decided to accept Michael's proposal.

Michael summarized his marriage: "Probably my best eleven years."

And for almost six of those, he had been coping with ALS.

Because it lay at the heart of many of Michael's stories, much of his memoir became about how he chose to deal with ALS. The stories I selected served to demonstrate how he had rationalized its severe limitations on him. His memoir was not about ALS, though. It was about how ALS showed exactly who he was—Michael's way of being.

When I asked him how and when he learned he was living under the death sentence of a rare disease, Michael was factual and candid as usual.

"Michael, can you recall when you first felt that something was wrong, when you first were aware of the disease?"

He didn't hesitate. "The first time I noticed that there was something different was when I was in the basement where I have a little trapeze set up for myself. I'd get on a little stool and hold onto the trapeze and dangle to stretch my back out. I'd gone to a chiropractor years ago and he'd said that every once in a while, I should stretch out a little bit to keep my back loosened up. So I'd hang from the trapeze for maybe a minute, two minutes, at a time.

"But this time, I could only hang on for not even ten seconds. My hands seemed to slip right off. I tried several more times, but I just couldn't hold on to grip that trapeze. That was the first sign that something was wrong. That was more than five years ago."

"What did you do about it? Did you go to the doctor to find out what was wrong?"

"No. I just thought maybe it was temporary."

"So what happened to finally get you to the doctor?"

"The second time I noticed something was when I went to shave and I'd hold the razor up for maybe fifteen seconds and suddenly my hand would fall straight down. I just couldn't hold my hand with the razor up to my face to shave. Eventually I started to use two hands to shave—one hand to hold the other hand."

Ellen joined in. "He told me about it then, and I said, 'Mike, there is something wrong somewhere.' And do you know what he said to me? He said it was just old age. But I insisted. He can be a little stubborn, especially about himself. And he went by himself, and he didn't even see the doctor."

"So what happened, Michael?"

"I'd been going to a physician's assistant for colds and things like that, and so I went to see her. After I explained, she said, 'I think you're just getting old. Elderly people lose their flexibility, and so on. That's probably all it is.'

"Then I came home and told Ellen and she said, 'I don't believe her. It's more than that.'"

Ellen followed up on her suspicion.

"This time, *I* made the appointment with our family doctor … And I went with him too."

"So we went to my family doctor," Michael continued. "He examined me and I told him everything, and he said, 'I think we might have to have you examined by a neurologist. We'd better just get you checked out.' He sent me down to a neurologist in Tarentum, and that doctor did nerve conduction studies on my back. When we got finished he said, 'I think it's Lou Gehrig's disease.'"

Michael started to continue.

"Wait a minute. What about your reaction to the news? Did you understand about what having ALS meant?"

"Well, I follow baseball, and I knew that Lou Gehrig passed away from it. He lived several years after he was diagnosed with it. So I knew that it was fatal, but that for some people it took a longer time than with others. I knew that, more or less."

I asked Ellen if she was with him in the room at the time.

"Um humm. He just checked Mike all over from head to toe, same as what [later a specialist] would do, more or less. When he told us, I didn't take it too well. Mike did, though—he took it real well. Of course I broke down, but Mike has always been the stronger of us two."

Michael tried to blunt the emotionality that hung in the room. "You know, it was funny because we had a ramp built out by the side of our house, and I'd always said to Ellen, 'Now whenever you get to the point where you can't get up the steps, I'll be able to push you up in a wheelchair.' And here it turned out the other way around. It's been her pushing me up that ramp in my wheelchair."

With that, Michael gave a little laugh. Then, satisfied he had done what he could to break the tension, he continued.

"Yep, the neurologist didn't beat around the bush or anything. He said anything we need, just contact him, and he'd try to do everything he can to ease the process. We really like him."

Dealing with ALS was of greater interest to Michael than the disease itself. And by "dealing with it" I mean physically, not emotionally. As he told his stories of coping, I wondered what I would do in his position. By the time I finished with Michael, having listened to him for many hours for more than a month, I thought I knew.

"When I was first diagnosed with ALS, my arms went slack, and when I would walk around, they would just hang down limp from my shoulders. That put a lot of strain on my shoulders and my neck. It hurt and I couldn't really move them at all to ease the strain.

"I'd gone to a doctor near Pittsburgh where there is a medical center for help. I went to him and I told him my problem and he said, 'Well, I can fix you right up.' He got me a kind of strap to go around my neck on each side and down to my waist and he put slings on it so I could put my arms in and he said, 'Now that's going to work real well for you.'

"I had it on for about an hour, and because of the weight of my arms, my neck got so sore I had to take it off. I just couldn't wear it.

"When I came home I had an idea. Ellen and I went to a sporting goods store and I found a big, wide belt that is like a back brace. I also bought some ankle weight cuffs that runners use to train. I took the weights out and I hooked the cuffs onto the belt. With the belt on, I was able to slip my hands into the cuffs, so that all the weight of my arms was on my waist through the belt and not sitting there on my neck.

"When I went to visit the ALS specialist in Pittsburgh, he looked at my rig and wondered what it was. After I explained it, he said, 'Wow. That's a pretty good idea. Can I take a picture of it? I just might know some people that this might help.'

"So now whenever we go back to see him he asks, 'Well, what did you invent this time?'"

That was the first of many stories that Michael told me about how he devised "workarounds" in living with the increasing limitations of ALS.

More than once, I thought, *This guy would have made a great engineer.* Most of his stories showed real ingenuity in getting whatever he wanted done. For instance:

"We have a dog, Gabby, and whenever groundhogs would come around to eat my vegetables, she would chase them. But sometimes the groundhogs are smart enough they would climb a tree. They'd get pretty high up there where she couldn't reach them. So she would just lie on the ground and just keep watch.

"Well, I have a .22 rifle and I'd go out and I'd shoot the groundhog as it hid in the tree.

"But with the ALS, my arms got to the point where they were not muscular enough to hold the rifle up to get a shot at them. So I figured that if I lay on the ground and put the butt of the rifle at my shoulder, I could take my foot and lift the barrel of the rifle up in the air high enough to get a good shot.

"I shot one out of a tree that way." For Michael, that was the end of the story, but not for Ellen.

"I looked outside, and there he was, lying on the ground with the gun held up with his leg. I ran out and yelled to him, 'Mike, you could shoot your foot off!'

"It's just like him to think like that: 'Can't use my arms, so I guess I'll use my legs.'"

I wrote many more stories of Michael Chapman's ingenuity in dealing with the losses of ALS into his memoir. The theme of all of them is consistent: Michael did not surrender to ALS. He did not lament about his losses to it. He did not withdraw. Instead, he treated the disease as just another thing that comes along in life he was forced to deal with. So he dealt with it, and kept moving on. He relegated the dreaded Lou Gehrig's disease to the category of nuisance. What kind of man could do something like that? That was the question I tried to answer.

Part of it was his deep-seated morality, his sense of right from wrong and his insistence on the former. Perhaps an example can illustrate.

Michael and Ellen had to pay a lot of healthcare bills out of their own pockets. To get a little money, they had to sell off the timber from some of their land. An Amish fellow had come out to do the surveying, but they decided to take the offer of another company. Feeling that the surveying work should be compensated anyway, they called the fellow up and paid him $200 for his help even though he was full time company employee. They just didn't feel right getting something for nothing.

"And he's stayed in contact with us just out of appreciation."

Ellen added: "He just now came back again and saw us. Just in late August. He came up and said, 'If there's anything I can do for you folks, please let me know.' Then he said he was having his friends pray for Mike. He thinks a lot of us. He is just a very honest person."

Sometimes, in case there's something I've overlooked, I ask my writing partners one last question acknowledging the reality that they are near the end of their journey. I ask such a personal question only after having spent many hours with them. That way, I'm never asking it of a stranger.

"Michael, I'd like to ask you one more question. I'm just looking for the first thing that comes to mind: How do you feel about the fullness of your life?"

Usually the answer requires at least a little time for introspection. But with Michael, it was different. Without any hesitation at all, Michael Chapman answered, and as usual, his answer was clear, detailed, and direct.

"When I was about twenty years old, in my own mind, I had structured out my whole life.

"I thought I knew exactly what the steps were going to be in my life. And I have more or less followed them. I knew that I wanted to get an education. And I accomplished that. I wanted to get a decent job. And I accomplished that. And I figured that about the age of 35 or so, I would get married.

"But also I had it in mind that when my mother and dad got elderly that I would help take care of them. And I was able to do that. And I also wanted to own something. So I bought myself a car and a house, and that was what I wanted to accomplish.

"And after all that, I finally did get married. And I was glad I waited until I met Ellen. I saved the best for last."

It was a rational, straightforward answer delivered without grieving. I was surprised by what Michael had said, that he had essentially planned his whole life, but I was more impressed that he mentioned neither his ALS nor his coming death. He'd planned his work, then worked the plan. I've done literally hundreds of detailed plans for companies, products and even whole technologies. But it never crossed my mind to plan my *life*.

In finishing the Epilogue to Michael's memoir, I tried to sum up my feelings about working with him. I knew that I wanted to say something about the rapport I'd had with him. But it was, after all, not my memoir but his, and I knew him to be a religious man, so here is some of what I wrote:

"Michael chooses to make light of the situations that ALS has put him in. He *chooses* to not let his dependence on others depress either himself or them. That a man who had spent so much of his life as a solitary, independent person could find humor in the extraordinary dependency on others that ALS forces on its victims is quite striking.

Those of us who have had the good fortune to know Michael Chapman, would naturally agree that for Michael, a certain well-known prayer has been answered. And the answer is obvious.

Lord, please
Grant me the strength to change what I can change,
The courage to accept what I cannot change,
And the wisdom to know the difference."

Always keeping my own beliefs out of it, I do deal with their faith in writing partners' memoirs, especially if they talk about it at length. When I think they would make a religious reference in talking, I make it for them in their memoir. In particular, the over-quoted prayer above, seen on coffee mugs, greeting cards, wall plaques, and other sorts of religious memorabilia, has become trite for some. For me, however, the prayer seemed apropos in describing Michael Chapman. And I was pleased that the Chapmans chose to leave my Epilogue in the half-dozen copies of Michael's memoir that I prepared and gave them to distribute to family and friends.

* * *

I worked with Michael Chapman on his memoir in the summer of 2014—as luck would have it, a high point in America's awareness of ALS.

The so-called Ice Bucket Challenge started as a dare to either make a contribution to the ALS Association or receive a deluge from an ice water bucket. It quickly morphed into doing both, well documented on social media. The origin of the challenge is unclear, but the results are not. The ALS Association raised $115 million in August alone, more than double the contributions for all of the previous year.

Then, on September 6th the annual Walk to Defeat ALS was held in Pittsburgh.

Never having done a walk for any cause, I decided to do one now.

I walked for Michael Chapman, who himself had done the walk for five years, but who was no longer able to walk at all. His group was called "Mike's Soles," a pun that underscored the relationship of many of his walkers with Michael's church.

It was sobering to be with so many others walking and wheelchairing along in the various stages of ALS paralysis. I could see in them a broad spectrum of emotions from tears to jubilation to bravado. And I could see in them a living history of Michael's own physical deterioration.

In November, yet another ALS-related event brought my mind back to Michael. Christmas day of 2014 was to be the release date for *The Theory of Everything*, a movie biography of British astrophysicist Stephen Hawking. Michael Chapman knew of him, as both a fellow mathematician and a fellow ALS victim. A trailer for the movie prompted a grim thought: Michael was unlikely to live to see the movie.

Yet I knew the movie was likely already completed.

How could Michael get to see the movie?

I contacted everyone I knew who might help. Efforts with the movie's distributor and production company were in play when Ellen called on November 28. Michael had at last succumbed to ALS.

* * *

At Welch's Funeral Home in Ford City, Michael Chapman, who, before ALS, had done everything to avoid people's attention, was now the center of it.

This was a "Steelers Sunday" and in spite of the increased local frenzy of the televised NFL game as the playoffs approached, and even though the game itself was already under way, the funeral parlor was packed. I'd had to negotiate a long line for more than an hour to get to talk to Ellen and to make my farewell to Michael. I wondered what he would have made of drawing such a crowd.

As I thought back over Michael's memoir project, I realized I'd gotten involved as more than a writer—more than a hospice volunteer as well. And to boot, Michael's memoir itself wound up being more than twice as long as most. Something had drawn me in deeper.

Michael Chapman, a meticulous man of scrupulous independence who lost all of that to the necessities of ALS, seemed to have something people wanted to see—to witness. And there, standing beside his coffin, I began to realize what it was. Michael Chapman had a *unique* kind of courage. And all these people had come as much out of admiration of that as remembrance of the man who had lived it.

Just as I had.

I'd seen a lot of myself in Michael. Like him, I prefer to handle most things alone, relying on my own inventiveness and capability to solve problems and get things done. And I, too, enjoy the solitude of the great outdoors, even if I prefer hiking to tractoring.

But thinking deeper, in Michael Chapman I saw a model of how, when it comes time for me to face my *own* mortality, I too, should be able to do so calmly, thoughtfully and consciously. I came to understand that it is possible to relegate death to what it is: simply the last tiny bit of the beautifully broad entirety of a life. Understanding that Michael Chapman had managed to put death in its proper place, I realized that I should be able to do so as well.

By the time I wrote for Michael, I'd seen quite a few people deal with impending death. And I'd supposed that the most courageous was a woman who had suffered even longer under a fatal diagnosis. Jeannie Forbes had fought off a pernicious cancer for sixteen years—fifteen longer than her prognosis. Yet even at the end, when she was moved to the inpatient hospice unit, she still was hoping to get out for yet another new, experimental treatment. This is sort of courage that movies are made about—the courage of Dylan Thomas' famous poem *Do Not Go Gentle into That Good Night*. But it was not the kind of courage one would ascribe to Michael Chapman.

Leaving the crowded funeral parlor, I came to understand that to bridle my own death, all I would need is what Michael Chapman showed everybody.

A special kind of courage. *Not* the courage to resist misfortune. But the courage to accept it, yet never permit it to change you.

Journey: Evangelizing Hospice

I hoped I could change things for others who might find themselves in situations like the one Frank and I had endured. For those approaching life's end, I saw the disparity between hospital and hospice as a serious issue, and I thought that I could help them and their loved ones give it the serious attention it required. And I felt I could best make my argument by centering it on the contrasts between hospice and hospital care.

Sitting down at my desk, I tried to look at the differences logically and dispassionately. I worked them out on paper first. Next, I tried to think of possible solutions—concrete, actionable solutions. I sorted through those and picked the best idea. Really, it simply centered on the notion that the hospital needed to ease the passage of at least some of its terminal patients—to treat them differently from those who could and would get well. I came up with an idea I thought was pretty good.

But having an idea accomplishes nothing by itself. So I made an appointment with the director of nursing at Frank's last hospital to share my thoughts and my logic for a practical solution.

As I entered her office, with all the sincerity I could, I thanked the director, praising her staff for their work. I tried to emphasize that I was not there to complain, but to help her to meet the special needs of the dying and their loved ones. I mentioned that shortly after Frank's death, I had taken a tray of pastries to the nurses who had cared for him in gratitude for their efforts. From their surprise, I saw it was an unexpected gesture—especially once they learned that Frank had died.

It would have been easy for me to simply present my list of the differences between the hospice approach and the hospital approach to the director and claim that additional training was needed for her staff. But I'd analyzed the situation a lot more than just drawing that obvious conclusion. I knew that wasn't a very realistic solution. I knew that the hospital was a business, and I understood that the cost and logistics to implement such a large training program would make such a solution impractical, at least in the short term. Even so, I knew that people were dying in that large hospital every day, and it was likely that many of those families never heard of hospice. Like Frank, patients and families might suffer needlessly until a budget and a training program could be established. I guessed that might take months, if not years.

So I suggested a faster solution to the nursing director. I'd reckoned that one hospice nurse could be added to each shift. That nurse could go around to each patient in the hospital who was terminal, check records and charts and ensure that they were being treated as someone who was dying, not someone whom the hospital was trying to heal. That's all. I suggested that a hospice-trained and experienced nurse be an *advocate* for the dying patients—the role I'd had to assume for Uncle Frank.

Reasoning that the idea would take a little selling, I emphasized to the director that I knew a hospital is a business. And so I stressed the cost savings that eliminating unnecessary treatments and procedures could bring.

Pleased with myself, I thought I'd presented a good, actionable, and maybe even financially attractive solution to the problems I saw that the hospital had had in dealing with Uncle Frank.

I was with the director for nearly an hour. She was very attentive and seemed to be actively interested. As I finished up, I felt that she thanked me with sincerity, saying that it was rare that anyone would be so thoughtful about such a situation as to even suggest how it might be realistically improved. She told me she would consider what I said and re-read the documents I gave her that detailed my observations and suggestions.

Satisfied, I left her office with a smile and feeling a little better. I thought I might just make a difference—that Frank's and my troubles might at least result in something that could help others.

But what actually happened was that I got a phone call from the hospital's lawyer the next day. How naïve I'd been in simply trying to help.

But as to my idea itself, later a friend who worked in a similar hospital run by the same organization told me that it would never be implemented because it might create conflict over who was in charge of the patient. The time-honored system was that only one nurse on a shift had that responsibility and only doctors could interfere with it. I was told that such is the nature of a hospital's hierarchy. I'd proposed a change to "the system." And the system had been in place for a very long time.

I'd learned another lesson, but I could not leave it at that.

I still was determined to help the people who might be mired in the situation I had found myself in with Uncle Frank. I had to acknowledge that trying to change "the system" was something that I was not qualified to do. Then, too, I was simply not enough of a crusader to swim upstream against such a strong bureaucratic current. Even so, I knew I was right: there was a problem with how the hospital had handled a dying patient.

However, as I thought about it further, I saw there was another way to look at the problem. I could have initiated moving Frank to a hospice more than a week before I did. I simply wasn't aware of the option. Perhaps seeing the problem as a lack of awareness of hospice might yield a different sort of solution.

I made an appointment to see Anna Olszewski, the volunteer coordinator at the Good Samaritan Hospice where Frank had briefly been, and I told her my story. After a little thought, Anna suggested that perhaps I could champion hospice to potential patients, their families, and their caregivers directly. Anna welcomed me to speak as a volunteer hospice advocate. She said the hospice got requests for such speakers from time to time.

I thought that over. As my career had progressed upward, I'd increasingly had to overcome my dislike of standing in front of groups, especially large groups. I remembered the first time I'd had to speak to a room of more than 300 people. I'd had to do some deep breathing and centering exercises before I got up there. Over time, it had gotten easier and had become a big part of my responsibilities eventually.

But now I was being asked to speak about a field I was not a professional in. Now I was being asked to speak about hospice. In the far future, I would eventually become a Certified End of Life Professional, but back then, I was just a technology manager who wanted to help people.

Anna saw my concern and put it to rest. "Well, we wouldn't want to put you anywhere that asked for a talk that needed such a person, Richard. We'd be careful in sending you to speak. How about if we say you're only going to talk about your personal experiences? Does that appeal to you?"

That rang true. I could simply tell people what hospice had meant for Uncle Frank—and for me. Maybe this was something I could actually do to help people to avoid the nightmare Frank and I had been through. While it might not affect as many people as quickly as changing "the system," it was *something* tangible I could do to get a little positive value of what Frank and I had been through.

But first, I had to become a formal volunteer for the Good Samaritan Hospice. The process included a background check and lengthy training, including a number of written quizzes. The hospice takes its role seriously —and acknowledges that volunteers are part of it. While I did not yet see myself as someone who would actually have contact with hospice patients, I was to be a badged volunteer representing the organization, and I had to go through what was required of all volunteers.

So it was several months later that my first outside speaking opportunity came along. I was asked to be a guest on a talk radio program about healthcare.

WISR, an AM station in Butler, Pennsylvania, bills itself as news/talk/sports radio. I was asked to participate in a noontime, one-hour talk program entitled "Health Connection." The anchor on the program, Scott Briggs, was the emcee.

On a cold and snowy January, more than four months after Frank's death, Scott introduced his radio audience to the topic of the show this way.

"Good morning, everyone. Welcome to another edition of *Health Connection* on 680 'wiser' radio. Our two guests today are here to talk about Good Samaritan Hospice. Roni Lucas is from

Concordia Visiting Nurses. And we have a special guest with us today as well. Richard Haverlack is going to tell his story about how Good Samaritan Hospice was there for him more from a personal perspective. I know that Roni is very good at talking about hospice, but we are really looking forward to hearing Richard's personal story."

Scott asked Roni to give the particulars about the Good Samaritan Hospice so that the audience had the necessary background about the institution and what it does. Sitting there in the soundproofed studio, Scott then turned his attention to me.

"Well, Richard, thank you for coming in today. First of all, as a family member who has had a recent hospice experience, we're sorry for your loss, but the information and experience you provide here might be extremely useful to others out there that may find themselves in the same situation as you. Please give us a little background."

"Scott, I appreciate the opportunity to be here because I wish somebody had had this conversation with me a long time before I absolutely needed to learn about hospice first hand—on an emergency basis. Because of the experience I had with my uncle at his life's end, I've tried to make that into something positive, and I'm trying to talk to as many people as I can about hospice so that they can understand that there is a way to ease the transition that every one of us has to go through. And that the sooner that they start considering it, the easier it's going to be when the time comes. That is, looking into hospice care right now is not only going to make it easier for the dying person, but for the persons making the decisions about their care as well."

And then I told Frank's story, giving details about his last two weeks. Scott looked surprised and broke in several times for clarification. I noticed he, like me, was careful not to criticize the hospital. A couple of times, I had to take a second or two to get control of my emotions when still vivid memories got the better of me.

Scott was particularly interested in how I came to consider hospice. "Tell us about that. You say you were in an emergency situation—a last-minute thing, and we'd like some background."

"You will get any number of conflicting opinions and medical advice as you approach the point of hopelessness. And really I did not have hospice as an option in my own mind until several days before my uncle's death, when a social worker at the hospital finally told me that this was something I should be considering. I just had not had it in my mind up to that point. I knew the word existed. I had an idea of what it meant, but while you are in the healthcare environment of 'Gee, maybe if we do this, or maybe if we do that,' it is was not mentioned to me. And all the while, it was the one option that I ought to be considering, because there is a process to go through to get into hospice care, and it takes time like any other process. So what happened was I wasted the most valuable thing my uncle had then, which was the time he had left."

We went on to talk about the hospice care itself and the people whom I met there. And we wrapped up with Roni giving the website address and twenty-four-hour hospice hotline number that listeners could use to get more information and request a visitation from Good Samaritan personnel for enlightenment or evaluation.

And then the hour was over. Roni and I left the station with Scott's thanks and his promise to send a CD recording of the program. And he told us he would forward any inquiries that came in as a result of our live broadcast.

I got the CD of the radio program in a week. Even though Scott had encouraged the audience to call in, there hadn't been a single phone inquiry about hospice during or after the program, his note said.

I'd been told that Scott's program enjoyed a pretty good daily following. But now I wondered if the audience could grasp the fact that something like Frank's and my situation was actually going to happen to them personally… That it wouldn't "*maybe* happen," but "*definitely* happen?"

I knew they'd heard, but had they listened?

The next opportunity I got to try to increase general public awareness of hospice was from a Pittsburgh church group who had a monthly meeting to help enlighten their members about healthcare issues. The group had called the hospice and Anna sent along their contact information to me. I thought it would simply be a matter of picking a time and place and length of presentation. But when I contacted her, the group's coordinator seemed strangely reticent about my participation.

I had already developed a speech and visual presentation for a professional group I'd talked to at Concordia. They were healthcare coordinators of the north Pittsburgh area. A lot of my talk centered on the details of all of the unnecessary care that Frank had gotten in the hospital while he could have been in hospice. All of the vital signs taken at all hours, the meals that showed up only not to be eaten, the antibiotics unnecessarily administered, and the painful turnings they did to him in his bed, as well as the more subtle things like how the pain management meds were administered and when. I totaled all of this up over Frank's two-week stay, and it was a formidable listing. The closing I had devised squarely put myself—my ignorance of hospice—as the problem. I criticized no one else. And I finished with a call to action, asking the audience to help me "evangelize" hospice.

I'd gotten a standing ovation from the roomful of professionals who worked in hospice and end-of-life care situations. Then, after my presentation, several of the audience came up to give me personal encouragement to give the speech wherever and whenever I could. So I thought I was well prepared to give an interesting and informative talk to the church organization.

But unexpectedly, when I had her on the phone, the coordinator from the group would not even commit to have me speak at all. Instead, she said she needed to see what I would talk about.

Curious but cooperative, I emailed my PowerPoint presentation to her.

The next week I tried to contact her, but she did not return my call. I waited another week and tried again. No luck. When I finally got her, I asked if she needed any more information.

"I don't think so," she said. "I had a look at your presentation about the hospice and I'm afraid that I found it to be too one-sided."

Did I hear right?

"Uh, I guess I don't understand."

"Well, you only talk about the positives of hospice."

"Uh… I guess that I think for a dying person, I can't imagine any negatives to hospice. For their family either."

"Well there *are*. What about when they hasten the death of the patient?"

Now, by this time I had audited the Psychology of Death and Dying course taught at the University of Pittsburgh. So I was aware there was, in some radical quarters, the absurd notion that hospices are "death shops" that practice euthanasia. Nothing could be further from the truth. Hospices are places that revere life and who see dying as part of the fullness of a life and who want that part to be as positive and as serene as it can possibly be—for both the patient and for their loved ones as well. So I said:

"That's a peculiar statement. I'm wondering where you heard it."

"I didn't *hear* it. I *lived* it. My mother was put in hospice care last year, and I'm certain that they killed her with an overdose of morphine."

In the weeks of Frank's dying, nurses, both in the hospital and in the hospice, had given Frank small doses of morphine as well as other drugs to ease his pain.

"If you don't mind me asking, why are you so sure?"

"I'm a registered nurse and I've worked in a hospital for ten years and if anybody knows about such things, I do."

Uh-oh. This is getting worse.

"Ma'am, I am not a healthcare professional, and I'm sorry about your mother, but I've had a hospice experience that could not be further from what you describe. In fact, when I asked about things like morphine there I learned a lot about it and how the various ways it can be administered work. I think that, at least in my experience, the hospice nurses knew much more about morphine and its administration than the nurses I talked to while my uncle had been in the hospital."

"You are not qualified to make such a statement."

Bad move. I'm finished.

"Ma'am, you're right, of course, but I'm just talking about my personal experience. And I think if you have a look at my presentation again, you will see that it is just about that: the specifics of the things my uncle encountered in the hospital versus what happened in the hospice. I'm not trying to indoctrinate anyone. I'm simply trying to motivate them to learn more about hospice for themselves before they, too, are faced with what I was faced with—either for themselves or for a loved one."

"Well, even so. It's one-sided and does not talk about the risks of hospice care. I want our members to get the complete picture."

For the dying, how could the "risks" of being cared for by specialists in dying be greater than the risks of being cared for by those who see death as failure?

I wanted to shout this. Instead I said, "I'm sorry, but really all I'm prepared to do is to talk about my own experience."

"Well, I'll look over your presentation again, and we will call you if we decide to hear your talk."

I heard from her exactly when I expected to. Never.

I had not anticipated anyone actually being hostile toward hospice. And she was a nurse! But the next opportunity I got to speak about my hospice experience was even more surreal.

I was asked to talk to a group that I was sure would be more than casually interested. I was to speak to the Western Pennsylvania Parkinson's Foundation forum, a group for family and patients with that terrible disease.

I knew that Parkinson's disease is incurable. In itself, it is not fatal, but the disabilities, both physical and mental, that it produces are likely to be. Average of death after diagnosis is less than fifteen years with confinement to bed coming years before that. There is treatment to lessen symptoms (jerky tremors and loss of balance to name only two), and it might take years to run its course, but Parkinson's simply cannot be cured—it is diagnosis of a downward spiral toward death.

Feeling that people and their families who had to face up to the certainty of long-term lifestyle decline would be interested, I was hopeful I could persuade them to learn about hospice before they were forced to make inevitable end of life care decisions.

Excited by the prospect, I arrived early for my talk, scheduled in the evening so that working loved ones could attend. But as the time for the meeting approached, I became increasingly worried.

At five minutes to the hour, I went out to the table where a volunteer was checking people off and making name tags for them.

"Say, it seems that the attendance is not going to be too good tonight."

"Yes, it does seem really light. We have an informational meeting each month and it looks like this one hasn't attracted much interest. But, hey, we published it in our newsletter and mailings as we always do. So I guess there just isn't very much interest. But boy! You should have been here last month! We were mobbed. People even showed up who weren't members. It was held right here, too."

"That's odd. Do you happen to remember what the topic was?"

"Sure I do. It was a researcher from the medical school. He was giving a talk about the progress on the latest research they were doing for a cure."

Of course! The slender hope for a cure.

I had learned the Kubler-Ross stages of grief. I knew that the first, and perhaps strongest, is denial. Even though Parkinson's patients had a degenerative disease, these folks seemed disinterested in learning about how to make dying as comfortable and tranquil as possible. I'd been certain that since the membership included both patients and their families, there should be quite a few interested in hospice. But then again to do so, they would have to acknowledge that they actually *were* going to die.

Oh, well.

I gave my presentation to the handful of people who showed up. There were no questions. Evangelizing hospice to the general public was not going the way I'd hoped. My plan to enlist audiences to spread the word was fizzling.

But my most traumatic speaking experience was yet to come.

I was asked to talk to the staff at a local hospital—*not* the one where Frank had been a patient. A group of doctors, nurses and other hospital staff wanted a story about the hospice experience. It was to be a large group, and I was pleased. Maybe I could motivate them to suggest to patients and families that they look into hospice care as soon as they could. I wanted them to simply suggest the hospice option early to those in need, like I wished someone had done for me. Get them interested in learning.

My presentation turned out to be one of a series of monthly talks about real-life patient experiences. Even though it was scheduled at 7 a.m., the audience was large because attendance was required. It seemed like an ideal opportunity.

Things started off OK, through my recounting of Frank's and my journey. As I usually do, I started with an absurd, but true, icebreaker: "My uncle Frank was killed by his false teeth." It always gets a laugh, and hopefully tweaks up interest as well.

But as I went on, the audience, doctors, nurses, and aides grew more and more restless as I left the description of Frank's condition and how it came about. That's when I begin to contrast hospital with hospice. Even though I took pains to say it wasn't so, my audience seemed think I was complaining as I reiterated all of the unnecessary things that had been done to Frank and the contrasting serenity of the hospice.

I heard some muttering in the audience. Then, abruptly, several men in scrubs got up and strode out. They did not get to hear the part where I accepted full responsibility. Even more sadly, those leaving missed the part where I asked them to help others like me to look into hospice before circumstances demanded it. All I wanted was for them to simply suggest that families begin to think about it in cases where they judged that the patient was probably not going to recover.

All this happened even though I was well within the allotted time. All this happened even though I'd been warmly welcomed. All this happened even though I made it explicit that I and no one else was to blame.

Somehow, the hospital professionals seemed *offended,* even though Frank had not even been in their personal care at all

As I left that hospital I ran the experience through my head. Some who stayed to the end shot hostile looks. And I had criticized no one and nothing except myself for not having known about the hospice alternative. Yes, I did put a call to action in there, counting the people in the room and calculating how much could be saved if each of them talked to just five people in situations like mine. I had believed that healthcare professionals would understand that they are the main, if not the only, source of information for terminal patients and families. By simply giving hospice as an option as soon as possible, instead of when it was the last resort, they could save a lot of time, anguish and expense for everyone involved, including themselves.

And to top it all off, at the end of my talk, I was not invited back by the moderator as I had been told I would surely be when I first phoned the administrator in charge of the meeting.

Again, my plain message to simply *foster* hospice awareness was rejected.

But this time by professionals.

As I drove away from the bustling medical center, glumly I thought about my failure at evangelizing hospice. Cruising up the expressway, I gradually came to the conclusion that if potential hospice patients and their families themselves were not wanting to learn about hospice, and if the professionals who came in contact with them were not to be motivated to suggest that they do so, then I was wasting everybody's time—including my own.

Among the dying and the professionals who are caring for them, it simply seemed that no one wanted to hear about, much less prepare for, death.

Dejected, I pulled out my cell phone and called the Good Samaritan Hospice to make an appointment to see the volunteer coordinator once more. I couldn't take this. I needed to tell her that the rejection I was getting at these public speaking engagements was just too disturbing for me.

It would turn out that telling Anna Olszewski about my disappointment would do much more than alleviate my frustration. It would ultimately lead me to work with a group that not only appreciates hospice, but who will earnestly tell anyone asking that they *love* it and the people working in it.

* * *

Anna came out to meet me at the door of the GSH administrative office as usual. And just as usual she wore a businesslike suit that was undoubtedly a holdover from her previous position with a healthcare employer. Anna had come to Good Samaritan for the more altruistic—and more casually dressed—atmosphere of hospice.

Briskly, as any very busy professional would, Anna ushered me back to her office. As always upon seeing her, I warmly recalled the memory of our first meeting. Anna had very carefully pronounced her name for me. With a practiced delivery, she told me that in Poland, Olszewski (she slowly pronounced it: ol-SHESS-key) is as common as Smith is here. Amused, I'd quietly told her that Polish names were no problem for me. My mother's maiden name was Piergalski, and the place where I'd been born was called Polish Hill, complete with a main street grocery proudly named *Olszewski's Market*.

As we took our seats, I described the unexpected rejection I'd been encountering in delivering the hospice message. "You know, Anna, I guess that I'm just not cut out to be a salesman. I don't have a salesman's personality. They get told 'no' most of the time and they just keep on going until they get a 'yes.' I don't have the ego to deal with all that rejection. In all my career, I've been a valued resource, I guess you could say. I'm not used to having something I think is important ignored."

Of course Anna was conciliatory, saying it was the message, not the messenger, that was what they objected to.

"I think I understand that. But I'm simply not getting the job done—I'm not getting the message accepted. I'm used to being successful. I'm used to feeling good about what I do, and I felt rotten every time I've failed to get this message across."

Anna's knowing nod signaled her understanding. I wanted to do something that had a good outcome—a positive impact on hospice and its mission. She knew of my personal situation with Uncle Frank and understood how it had brought me to need to *do* something.

Anna pursed her lips, then picked a tri-fold flyer out of the clutter. "How about this? We're launching our first *Camp Erin*, a stay-over, three-night summer camp for children who experienced a death in their lives. It will be really beneficial for them to come together with other kids who are grieving. It'll let them know they they're not alone. And I've got to pull the whole thing together in just a few months. Maybe you could help out with that."

"You know, Anna, I've not mentioned this before, but my wife and I have no children. That was not by choice, but that's the way it is. And because of that, I've never really been around kids. I don't know how to act with them. I guess you could say I don't know how to relate to them. And I think for something like the camp you're describing you're going to need people who can relate, maybe even bond, with those kids, right?

Her eyes softened. She seemed to understand how I felt about children, and more importantly, why.

Anna rummaged around on her desk once again, shifting papers and reports, and came up with a clipping from the local newspaper.

"Maybe there is something in *this*. Did you see this article? It's about someone working at another hospice, a for-profit one. It seems she's been writing stories with her patients." Anna handed the clipping to me.

As I scanned the article about a hospice nurse who wrote out short stories her patients told her, Anna went on, "You know, Good Samaritan might want to offer this kind of thing to our patients. It might be comforting for them, and maybe for their families too. And you did say you were taking some writing courses, right?"

"Yes. I've taken a handful of informal courses and actually right now I'm in the middle of an undergraduate nonfiction writing course at Pitt."

Anna took the article and put it on the photocopier. "Maybe you can contact the woman who is doing this. And I we certainly would like to explore something like it. Why don't you give it some thought?"

I called the hospice service that was mentioned in the article and asked if I could speak to the caregiver mentioned in it by name.

I eventually reached a woman who was her manager. "What is it that you want? Maybe I can help you."

"My name is Richard Haverlack and I'm a volunteer for the Good Samaritan Hospice. I saw the article about writing patient stories in the paper and my volunteer coordinator and I thought maybe I could do something like that for our patients. I was just trying to gather a little information on how it's done."

"I see… Well, maybe it would be best if I called you back, OK?"

I waited a couple of days, then I called once more and asked for the manager by name.

"Oh, yes. Time got away with me. Listen, we are careful about privacy, and we have decided that the woman in the article should not talk to outsiders about her work with the patients."

"Uh, I don't want any information about patients. All I want to do is to talk to her about how she does the writing that she does. You know, maybe get some tips from her."

"Well, the privacy I'm talking about is *her* privacy.'"

HER privacy? The woman's name and photo is in a newspaper.

Guided by my own business experience, I straightaway concluded that this for-profit company likely saw story writing as a sort of advantage. One to be guarded from a "competitor." But it kept that to myself.

"Uh, thanks. Sorry to have bothered you."

"Oh, no bother at all! And you have a nice day!"

Not being able to get any anyone else's, I thought that I'd ask my writing class instructor at Pitt what he thought about writing for hospice patients. I was a little apprehensive about doing such a thing. I'd been writing for most of my career, but that was technical literature. My own creative writing had been seen only by classmates and teachers. I had some doubts about my ability.

Graciously, since I was just auditing, Mark Kramer agreed to talk to me.

Hearing about my doubts, Mark thought for a little. "Well, maybe you could do a sort of trial run to see how it works out. I'm planning to have the class do a project that involves conducting a field interview, then writing a story about it. Although you're just auditing, I could manage an informal look at anything you might write."

"Would you really? That sounds great. Maybe I don't need guidance from anybody. Maybe I can come up with my own way of working."

In Mark's class we were going over interviewing skills, having already studied nonfiction writing and techniques—with lots of practice on lots of papers. I had written the papers like all of the formal students and was permitted to exchange them during our peer critiquing sessions. I suppose Mark thought it would be good for the undergraduates to get exposure to the writing of someone who was older. And I certainly enjoyed getting the points of view of writers who were one-third my age. It had worked out well both ways, I think, even though I'd overheard one of the students talking to a friend about "The Q-tip" in his writing class and the stories he wrote set back before they were born.

I scouted to find someone whose story I could write. I wanted to see whether I could actually interview someone a lot older than myself and get an interesting story out of it. I thought of whom I could interview. I ruled out actually working with a hospice patient. And I'm sure Anna wouldn't have let me experiment on one anyway. At Good Samaritan, everyone is aware of how precious the time remaining to the patients is. And the last thing I would want to do would be to cause anyone who was dying any additional emotional discomfort while I sorted myself out.

What I needed was someone older who could essentially act as a surrogate for the hospice patients whose stories I thought I wanted to write. No way a stranger would agree to such a fishing expedition. I'd have to find someone who knew me. With all of my parents' generation in my family gone, I had no idea who to approach.

Then, too, there was the daunting notion of the whole idea. I'd never done anything like this before. I'd made several successful careers in engineering. I certainly knew how to plan, analyze and execute complex projects. I'd honed those skills to a fine edge, but this was something different. This was coaxing information out of someone and then creating a story that others would find interesting enough to want to read. And it was interacting with a stranger much more intimately than I ever had. This was going to be as much about skills of listening as of writing.

It was going to be like entering another, totally different career.

But in this career, I'd not be a seasoned professional. I'd be a green newcomer.

A Writing Partner's Tale: *Listening*

To learn, you must first listen.
Anonymous

I record my immediate impressions of a writing partner as soon as I leave each meeting—usually, in my car as I drive away. Sometimes these recordings give me insight that might otherwise get lost as their stories unfold. Sometimes they provide information that makes the writing easier or richer in texture. And in rare instances, they expose a characteristic that later provides the focus for the entire work.

After our first interview, sweating in my car in the August heat, I struggled to say what, exactly, my first impression of Heather Lassen had been. I switched on the air conditioner and spoke up over its noise. My recorder captured words like "direct," "no-nonsense," and "precise." But these seemed somehow superficial. There was something else there. Something I could not put my finger on.

It would come to me, but only after some serious introspection reviewing our disastrous (at least for me) third interview.

Sometimes my volunteer writing for patients of the Good Samaritan Hospice requires more than the usual three interviews. With Heather, it took five, but the revelation of just what made Heather unique came in that third, most unusual, meeting.

Our talk was long—almost three hours. And as I recorded my exit notes from that meeting, I was upset. Not with Heather, but with myself. I realized that I had done an awful lot of the talking—maybe even most of it.

"The interview went off the rails," I said into the recorder. I was describing the last part of the meeting. Not only had I been speaking almost continually, but I also had been preaching my own viewpoint, something that has no place in trying to write someone else's story. I realized I'd strayed too far from getting Heather to tell me what was on her mind. I had to study the interview to figure out where things went wrong as soon as I could, and definitely before going to see Heather for a fourth visit.

At home that evening, I put on the earphones and played back the entire interview. It had started out fine, but by the end, something was awry.

Heather was interviewing me.

Playing the recording several times, I picked up the moment when the tables turned.

We were talking about Heather's religious views and her churchgoing history. Heather was born a Presbyterian, converted to Catholicism, then went back to being a Presbyterian. When her son was born, she decided he should be raised as a Catholic!

I was curious about all of this church-changing, and Heather didn't seem to mind talking about it. But as I listened again, I found that subtly, increasingly, Heather had begun to ask me questions. She smoothly slid in the first question about my own religious beliefs, tying it to something I'd said about her changing religions. In our first meeting, she'd said she was a Presbyterian but hadn't always been one, and I'd echoed that I, too, had become one later in life. Sharing significant life experiences like that increases bonding, a simple way to encourage conversation and something I do whenever possible with a writing partner.

But on this day, I could hear myself perk up in answering Heather's question about my own religious switch. She sensed this, I think, because she asked a follow-up question. And another. But I didn't notice any of that in the moment of the interview. My mind was now on *me*. Although I didn't realize it, *Heather* was beginning an interview that lasted more than thirty minutes. The audio plainly revealed that I had become the interviewee.

This had never happened with another hospice patient. Really, by this point in my volunteerism, my interviews amounted to more than 100 hours, so the table-turning was more than rare—it was remarkable. How had I let it happen?

Sitting there at my lamp-lit desk in the dark room, listening to the recording, I became increasingly unsettled, even embarrassed. This was not supposed to happen. I try to be professional in the interviewing and writing of patients' memoirs. I carefully watch the time. I stick to an outline and ask questions designed to stimulate detailed answers.

I was ashamed I had lost my self-control. Even more, I was ashamed to have used Heather's valuable time in such a way.

After listening to the interview and my expositions one last time, I did something that I'd never done before (and haven't since, for that matter). I edited the audio file. I cut out the portion where I talked too much so the interview CD I'd make for Heather and her family would not include it. The CD was supposed to be an audio memento of her, not me.

Chastened, on every interview I've conducted since then, I guard against losing self-control. My writing partner can go where they want. The interview can wander at their will. When I am tempted to pipe up, I remember that August afternoon with Heather Lassen, and I suppress my urges. I've since learned an acronym that can help me to stay out of the conversation: WAIT— Why Am I Talking?

With Heather, I knew that I'd spoken out because our interview had touched on a personal hot button. But there was more to it than that. Giving it a lot of thought, I realized that our role reversal was actually something that Heather Lassen had caused—had perhaps wanted to cause. And as it turned out, her maneuver was what gave me deeper insight into her character—a unique characteristic that could help the reader of her memoir to know her better.

I set aside my voice recorder, got up and began to pace. What had driven my interviewee to take such an active interest in me and my beliefs? She'd skillfully urged me on. One minute I'd been interviewing her, and the next I was spouting personal views that I hadn't shared with anybody—ever.

Turning that question over and over in my mind, it came to me at last. And it was so central I knew I would use it as the foundation for the voice I would use in writing Heather's memoir. It had been there all along, from our first meeting on.

Heather had been an elementary teacher for more than thirty years. And she had taught the most challenging of students, those with learning disabilities. She was renowned in her school system for getting results from children that others had had no success with. She had told me how she did it, too. She said she simply bonded with each student individually, not as a teacher, but as an equal.

I sat back down at my desk, and got out my notebook—the one I use during interviews. Slowly, leafing through the details I'd written about her, I began to realize that treating me like an equal—bonding with me—was what she had been doing all along in that day's interview. Perhaps it was what she did with everybody she had an interest in.

I'd been wrong about what had happened. It was not that Heather had taken control of the interview, it was simply that she had been expressing active and sincere interest in what I had to say, moreover, why I was saying it. That's what encouraged me to talk so much.

This is called *empathic listening*, where the listener strives not only to get information, but also to make an emotional connection to increase understanding. It is the highest, most engaged kind of listening you can do. It is about gathering what something *means* to the speaker in addition to what that something is. It is about emotion as much as information. And it is a powerful way to build a bond with someone.

I know this well because it is what I strive to do myself in interviewing hospice patient writing partners. I learned about it years ago from the book *The Seven Habits of Highly Effective People* by Stephen Covey, one of the all-time best sellers of its kind. I don't know where Heather learned to do it, but now I realized that in Heather's teaching she must have gained the trust and cooperation of her special needs students by practicing empathic listening. I concluded this because Heather had simply done the same with me. And it had worked.

As I thought about it further, I could see my impressions about her from our first interview back in August fit with that. She was a teacher, and at our first interview, she had wanted to establish herself as direct and no-nonsense. She was telling me that if she showed interest, it would be sincere. And so in our third interview, she had empathically listened to me and her sincerity subtly encouraged me to open up to her.

That was it. I had the right voice for Heather, the voice of an *empathic* teacher. And although I try to do the same for everybody I write for, getting to this point was doubly important for Heather's memoir in particular.

Heather said she wanted to use her story to give advice to her young grandchildren—lasting advice about what is important in life. Such a memoir would be too difficult to read if written in the third person. So even though I prefer not to write in the first person, now I felt that I could do it for Heather. I could tell her story like she would—I could organize the story and stress what the information she wanted. But most importantly, now I saw how I could make the work sound the way she would have sounded herself.

In her memoir, Heather wouldn't be telling. She'd be teaching.

* * *

As I usually do, I gave Heather a draft copy of the completed memoir with explicit instructions to change or even delete *anything* that did not sound right to her—anything that she would not say herself. The draft came back with only minor edits. Heather was pleased with what the work said and how it said it. Written by a teacher as loving advice to her grandchildren, who were themselves children of a teacher, it has sections of suggestions and observations. Here are excerpts of Heather's memoir summarizing what she feels is important in life. The teacher of exceptional children can easily be heard.

Listen and Observe. "You know how you feel when someone just seems to not understand you. Well, they feel the same way when you don't exactly get what they are trying to say." This was Heather's longest topic. She wanted it put first, too.

Assess the Situation. "Usually, doing the right thing is much more important than doing the fast thing. So slow down and think before you act."

Know Your Purpose. "It's important to set goals and remember to work toward them. That's the only way you know if you're getting to where you want to."

Take Action. "Judge others by what they actually do. You can see that if you agree with this, then you yourself should be judged not by what you think but by what you *actually* do."

Make Promises. "A promise is a good thing to do for two reasons. First, once you make a promise, you are much more likely to actually *do* what you said. ... The second reason is that when you do your very best to meet your promise—whether you meet it or not—people will see that you are the kind of person that they can trust."

Take Your Time. "More than the speed, it is the quality of the work that you do that will have the most to do with your success in life. ... And taking time is never more important than it is when you are dealing with people."

Keep an Open Mind. "You know that in my work with special needs children ... they were just different in their ability, not in their humanity. This is the worst thing that comes from *not* having an open mind: stereotyping. (Look it up!)"

Reach Out. "It is important to be the one that gives comfort. YOU need to be the one who reaches out, especially when others are not. You be the one to reach out first. It always works."

Be Sensitive. "Everyone has feelings. Unfortunately a lot of people go to great lengths to hide their feeling from others. ... [If someone hurts you] say the concern that is on your mind directly: 'That hurt me—did you really mean to do that?' You will be surprised at what this little phrase can do."

Laugh. "Laughter is the best way to calm any situation. Sharing laughter is the best way you can bond with anyone else, no matter who they are."

Then came a section that dealt with the topic Heather had gotten me to expound on. Even though she had so empathically listened to my view of religion, it's clear my thoughts in no way changed hers.

Religion. "You know that I have changed religions. But do you know that I have not changed my faith? A religion is an organized group who have some sort of common rules and ideals. Faith is what you believe inside. I knew about religious diversity from the beginning on. I grew up across the street from a Jewish synagogue and there our neighborhood had Catholics and Protestants in it, too. Since I knew that there were a lot of good people in my neighborhood, no matter what their religion, I never could see getting bent out of shape over religion, but by far one of the most significant things that I can tell you is that faith is really important.

"To me, faith is trust in God. I have faith, so I know that God will take care of you. But *you* need to have faith, too, so that you will know that things will be all right for you and for those you love. Faith has given me the strength to face some tough situations. It is faith that is helping me to get through my illness right now, even though I know that I'm not going to get better. I know, through my belief, my faith, that there is something afterward and that I will be OK. This is comforting. I can't imagine how it would feel to not believe this, to not have this faith. I have mentioned travel earlier as a way to learn about people and how they are different. Those differences extend to their faiths, of course.

"But again, don't mistake religion for faith. What people, individuals, make of their religion is their faith. You need to know a person well before you can comment on his faith, his beliefs. So be wary of the labels that the names of religions bring. Those labels make it sound like all people who practice a certain religion are alike, and by now you know that that just is not true.

"I'm not just trying to preach here. Faith is *real*. When I've had problems, God's always been there to talk to and to ask for help. It can be that way for you, too. All you have to do is pray from your heart. You will get the faith to see you through. When everything seems to be going wrong, there is always that place, that faith, *your* faith, that you can rely on to see you through. Please remember that. You never need to feel that you are at the end of your rope. You always have your faith to turn to. Nothing can take this away from you. So think about what you believe in. Seek out others, a particular religion if you want, that shares many of your beliefs, but know that faith is inside you, not in a church. And it is your faith that will always see you through."

Finally, Heather wanted to create a section to close out her memoir in a way that acknowledged her own death, and what she wanted her grandchildren to learn from it. We'd talked for a long time about how to do this. Working together, I think we came up with a great close.

As I typed Heather's words into the memoir, I could not help but think about what a wonderful gift she was giving them. Grandmothers occupy a special place in the hearts of young children, and that place is held special even as they grow to maturity. I still revere my grandmother, Rozalia Piergalska, and she will forever be held in my heart. Heather Lassen knew about this truth because she knew that all three of her grandchildren loved her dearly, and she was telling them—teaching them, really—how to get beyond her death. And she did it with sincerity and empathy because she had a clear understanding of who there were and how they saw things.

In writing the memoirs of hospice patients, I've encountered many objectives for the works we jointly create. And sometimes I get more involved with a memoir than just writing it. For instance, when I think it would be helpful to a writing partner, sometimes I suggest what they might consider including.

For its closing section, I asked Heather if a certain passage from the Bible would be good to include. Without hesitation, she agreed. She said she wanted to expound on it as a farewell. Heather's memoir of advice to her grandchildren is entitled *A Time for Everything,* and it ends this way:

> "A lot of wise men have written about this, about change, and how it comes to everything that there is—especially to every person that there is. The writing about change that I like best is this:
>
> 'To everything there is a season,
>
> And a time to every purpose under heaven.'
>
> [...]
>
> This passage, from Ecclesiastes, says what I want to say about change.
>
> Whatever is troubling you right now is temporary. It will change.
>
> That is inevitable. But how change affects you and what you do about change is not inevitable. It is up to you. For me,

my faith has seen me through some of the tough changes I have had to face. I think that faith can do the same for you. But whatever *you* choose to see you through hard times that you will face, I'm pulling for you … praying for you.

It is time to close this off now. As you read this in the future, I wish I could be there so that I could try to help you then, but I can't. I wrote this now to try to help you then.

I love you, and I've told you all of this here and now only because I want you to be happy always."

After Heather's memorial service at the Presbyterian Church in Saxonburg, her daughter-in-law came up to me and thanked me for my work. She went on to say that her children had been close to Heather and that their grandmother's death had been a great loss. And when their grief seemed overwhelming, she would take out Heather's memoir and read the ending aloud to them.

And I knew that ending for what it was: a lesson their grandma, an empathic teacher, wanted her grandchildren to learn.

Journey: Writing Ruth

I like to attend high-school football games. Most men roll their eyes when I talk about it—they only watch the college and the pro teams. High-schoolers just don't have the moves yet for spectacular plays, they say.

I don't watch high-school football for the results—the scoring and the plays. It's for the sincerity of the playing—the intensity of it. They play with heart.

On one chilly autumn evening after a particularly thrilling high-school game, I sat with a longtime friend over burgers and beer. I'd gone through elementary and high school with John Musser and we'd connected again later in life. John enjoyed the high-school games as much as I did. He was an avid follower of the local teams at all levels and in all sports. I pretty much only went to high-school football and basketball games to be in the moment. I followed no team, except maybe when the Steelers were doing well.

Our conversation rambled as it usually did. We were interested in each other's lives—both the similarities and the differences. So it was not unusual that the topic came around to my hospice volunteerism. John and I are pretty open with each other, so I told my story of foundering as an advocate speaker and set out my interest to move on to writing for patients. He paused when I mentioned I was looking for someone who could be a surrogate for the hospice patients I ultimately wanted to work with. Someone I could interview and write for on a joint writing project.

Ever thoughtful, John likes to help whoever and whenever he can. He didn't so much as pause. "How about my mother? She's 92 and still pretty sharp. I'll bet she'll remember you from back in high school. I'm not sure she'll like the idea, but if you want, I'll talk to her about it."

It sounded ideal. I remembered meeting Mrs. Musser way back, but I also realized *that* Mrs. Musser was now more than forty years in the past.

I was relieved when John called in a few days. Mrs. Musser had agreed to act as my guinea pig.

Mark Kramer's writing class at the University of Pittsburgh had taught me the importance of recording the dialogue during an interview, so I'd purchased a tiny digital recorder. After practicing with it a couple of times and going over my notes on interviewing, I finally found myself parked in front of "Camelot," Ruth Musser's condominium apartment building.

I looked over my notes yet again—especially the dos and don'ts of interviewing. Then, as the time of our appointment arrived, I sighed, packed up my notebook and recorder and made for the front door.

I can't believe I'm so nervous.

Mrs. Musser buzzed me in almost instantly—she must have been waiting. I wondered if she'd seen me out in the car while I sat there reviewing and reviewing my notes. I turned from the door and climbed the dozen steps to her floor.

Ruth Musser stood at the open door of her apartment. I recognized her immediately. Her jet-black hair had gone gray, and the glasses she wore were in keeping with today's style and not those of my distant memory, but she still looked very like the Mrs. Musser I remembered. She was slim and erect, and her face belied her age. I noticed she wore a trim white blouse and black skirt.

Did she dress up just for me?

"Hello, Mrs. Musser! It's good to see you after so long. Are you going out this afternoon?"

"No, why do you ask? I set aside the afternoon to talk to you. John told me about your project and I hope I can help," she said, ushering me into her apartment.

"Oh, sorry. You just looked like you were dressed to go somewhere, that's all."

"I always dress like this. And who would wear slippers to go out?"

I saw that she indeed had fuzzy slippers on her feet. And she was off, leading the way not at all with the tentative gait of advanced age. As I strode to keep up, I recalled that John had told me that she was still driving herself.

"Where would you like to sit? I see you have a big notebook. Maybe we'd best sit at the table."

She led me through the living room and into the dining alcove. I hadn't thought about where to interview her, so I simply followed. She sat down at the dining-room table and I took the opposite chair. For a moment we smiled at each other across the expanse of gleaming wood.

This feels uncomfortable—too formal.

But I started right in anyway to explain what I wanted to do. Telling her what I thought the process would be and how long I thought we'd need to talk and what I was going to do with the information and how much I appreciated her help.

Mrs. Musser laughed and raised her hand. "Wait a minute. Slow down! How are you? It's been quite a few years. And John said you needed some help with your writing, but I'd really like see how all this came about."

"Oh… Sorry."

A little sheepishly, I went through a brief career bio and I finished with a recounting of the story of Uncle Frank's coming to hospice, and how I hoped to write for hospice patients. I went on to explain the writing project for class that our talks were for. And I thanked her for agreeing to the interview.

"It will be a great help in seeing if I can actually do what I have in mind. I've not done anything like this before. The kind of writing I've been doing in my professional career is very technical. I've had several writing classes, but I haven't tried anything like writing from interviews before."

"Well, you certainly look the business part with your suit and tie and that big thick notebook." She chuckled. "And you grabbed that pen right out of your pocket even before you sat down!"

"Oh, I'm sorry to rush you. I really don't want to do that. I guess I'm a little nervous."

I put pen to paper and made my first note. "Be more casual and dress that way, too." Then, reflecting, "Sit somewhere comfortable and informal."

Mrs. Musser watched as I reached into my pocket and took out my brand-new recorder. I switched it on and set it down on the table. The red-light indicator showed that it was recording.

She frowned. "And what is that?"

"Oh, I'm sorry. I should have explained. I need to record the interview. It would be impossible to write all the details fast enough. Uh, that's OK, I hope?"

Mrs. Musser responded a little slowly, eyeing the small, black device. "Well, will anybody else hear it? I thought I'd just be talking to you."

"Uh, yes, I mean no, I mean I can promise that no one else will hear this."

"Well, what if I want to hear it?"

"Uh, well, sure."

I've got to make recording less of a threat somehow.

"Tell you what. How about if, when I'm done with the interview, I make a CD of the recording for you? You've got a CD player, right?"

"Yes. What did you think? That I'd still be listening to 78s?" she smiled again.

I smiled right back at the thought.

"OK, OK. But is it all right to use the recorder? No one else will get to hear it and I'll make you a CD to do whatever you want with. That OK?"

She thought for a while. "Yes. Maybe the boys will be interested in what this was about." She had two sons, I remembered: John and his younger brother, Larry.

I reset recorder, then thought to speak into it myself first.

"Well, it's the sixteenth of October 2008, and I'm here with Ruth Musser and we're going to talk a little about her life. And I hope she will be willing to tell me some stories."

"Stories? John didn't say anything about any stories. I thought you just wanted to ask some questions about me and I would answer."

In my notebook, I jotted: "Explain exactly what you want and why." Then I looked up at Mrs. Musser.

"I need you to tell me some stories that I can put in my essay. I mean I'd like to hear about more than just a factual account of where you've been and what you did. So maybe we can start with this: What is the most memorable thing you've ever done?" I thought that would help.

Mrs. Musser's brow beetled. "What do you mean?"

"Oh, anything that comes to mind—the first thing that pops into your head when you hear that question."

"Well nothing pops into my head. I thought I was going to tell you about my life."

"Yes, yes, that's just what I want to hear, what was memorable in your life."

"What was memorable in my life... I've never really done anything important."

"Oh, come on, sure you have," I prompted. "Just tell me what was most exciting for you."

"Exciting... Maybe this is not going to work out. I've just been a housewife and a mother. I've never done anything exciting, I'm afraid."

Don't panic!

"Maybe I'm not being very clear. Let's start again. I just want to hear about who you are, and where you've been, and whom you've met, and what you've done."

I was definitely panicking now.

"Richard, I don't know..."

"Look, I haven't started this off very well. Tell you what. How about if you just tell me about your life, starting with where and when you were born and just going from there as you remember growing up?"

"Oh. Well. That I can do, but as I said, I've led a pretty tame life. I've never done anything important at all. I was just a mother and housewife."

"Well, it will be good for me to hear about your whole life, I think. You lived through the Depression and the Second World

War and you were in the generation that created suburbia—where we all lived. I'd really like to hear about."

"Well, that sound grandiose. I'll talk, but don't be expecting anything fancy...

"Really, Ruth. May I call you Ruth? I'm just interested in hearing what things were like for you."

"Now that, I can tell you. My memory is still pretty good... Well, I was born in Harrisburg. My father was a postal worker. Our family was pretty solid German stock..."

I let out my breath. We'd finally begun.

I had started off all wrong, and I had almost blown it. Too rushed. Too unthinking, really. I'd asked Ruth to present me with the story jewels of her life. I'd rushed to get what I wanted even before she got to know who I was and why I wanted to talk to her. And I'd assumed she was prepared to give me what I wanted. I'd seen the whole thing through my eyes only.

After all, it was supposed to be about writing Ruth, whatever that might turn out to be.

As I later reviewed the day and the interview, I slumped before my laptop. I was transcribing the conversation verbatim— producing such a transcript was one of the requirements of Mark's writing project. Listening to how it had gone, dark doubt crept over me. Maybe I wasn't suited to be doing this for hospice patients after all. Maybe it wasn't going to work out.

I thought about the other students in the class: the animated girl who had said she wanted to interview a bartender about his job; the thoughtful fellow who said he was going to interview his parents' neighbor who was a city bus driver; and the bright kid who said he was going to talk to his cousin who was an EMS medic. Those students knew exactly what they wanted out of their interviews. And they were going to use it to write interesting and entertaining material. They were going to produce stories that others wanted to read.

But my own first interview is over, and I have no idea what I'm going to write about.

After I finished the transcription, I was still no closer to seeing a story. I snapped shut my laptop, went to the liquor cabinet, and poured bourbon over ice.

Oh, well. Writing for hospice patients had been a nice thought. But nobody said it had to work out.

I'd spent an hour with Ruth Musser on our first visit. I knew I'd have to get at least three hours of interview for the paper. So I'd made an appointment with her to continue.

As I prepared for our second interview, discomfited, I thought back on my performance. I was supposed to write *her* story and all I'd done was try to get her to give me one that I wanted. As I thought about it more deeply, maybe that was what you could do if you already knew the story you wanted to write—about bartender hijinks, about EMS cliffhangers. I realized that I simply did not yet know what the story I was going to write was going to be about.

In a moment of insight I realized a deeper truth. *Neither did Ruth Musser.*

Then I thought about how I'd behaved—but from Ruth Musser's point of view.

A stranger sits down in front of you and out of the clear blue asks you to tell him "interesting" or "exciting" stories. And just like he is some sort of confidante.

Too unexpected. Too much pressure. Too intimate too quickly.

Yet I could see that when Mrs. Musser had actually begun to talk about the familiar memories of her childhood and then to simply to build upon them further with others later in her life, she became more relaxed, receding and reliving the memory, no longer struggling to come up with something "exciting."

OK. So relax. Take it slow.

Start with the easy to remember, the familiar memories of childhood. Let her tell me the background of the story way ahead of the story, whatever it might be. Let it unwind. No need to rush. Have a little faith that a story about *something* will come.

And with Ruth Musser, on two subsequent visits, it did. And it was a story that I never expected. And it was a story that was unique. And it was a story that everyone would want to hear. It was a great story.

Really, Ruth's compelling tale began with a tiny thread she mentioned near the end of our first, ill-begun, visit:

"When I was young, my two older brothers used to take me to dances with them. It was the Big Band era—Benny Goodman,

Glenn Miller, those bands. I was too young to dance with the teenagers, so I would just go and stand right in front of the bandstand and listen while the older kids danced. I really went to a lot of dances though I was still too young to go dancing."

So in our second interview, when Ruth had finished talking about her life all the way up to the present, I tugged a little on that thread.

"You talked about the dances you went to with your brothers. You said you liked it a lot, so where else have you gone dancing, Ruth?"

"Well, when I was in high school, everybody danced. We had dances in the cafeteria at lunchtime a couple of times every week. You know, just a record hop kind of thing. I really liked them. And my first date with my husband was to a dance, a formal one."

She went on to describe her marriage, and their time together as her husband, Jack, was called up and trained for World War II. And then Jack was gone to England where he was preparing for the European invasion, and to follow the offensive across the continent in the field hospital he had helped to establish. He went all the way up to the final push into Germany.

Later, as I transcribed our second interview, when I got to this passage, I leaned back thinking about the young Ruth Musser of the wartime.

And what did you do while you waited out those war years, Ruth?

She had skipped over what the war years had brought her personally, giving instead a lot of detail about her husband and his wartime stories. So on our third meeting, I led with a question about how she had done in the years her husband was away at war.

And there was that thread again.

"Oh nothing. I worked and I moved in with my sister to help her take care of her two kids—her husband had gone off to fight, too, I think he went to the Pacific."

"Where did you work?"

"Oh, I was just a secretary at a steel company in Harrisburg."

"So what did you do there?"

"I handled personnel records. It was nothing really. Just a lot of filing and paperwork. Nothing that would interest anybody."

"Well it helped the war effort, you know. It took a lot of steel to win the war."

Then an afterthought: "What did you do when you weren't working?"

"I helped my sister with her kids. That was pretty much it."

"What about entertainment? I'll bet you went to the movies—Bogart, Betty Davis, all those great silver screen icons."

"Yes. We went whenever we could—on the nights when we didn't go to a dance.

What was that?

"Dance? Did you go to dances?"

"Oh, sure. Every Wednesday night there would be a dance at the base and I'd go and dance with the GIs."

"I didn't know there was an Army base in Pennsylvania."

"Oh, it was right outside of Harrisburg at Indiantown Gap."

In my era, Fort Indiantown Gap had become a National Guard base, so later I did some research. The fort, located near a major rail nexus just outside of Harrisburg, turned out to be a major training and assembly point for GIs heading to the war in Europe. It was there units were built up and sent via trains, then ships, to the European theater. It had been a giant operation. Thousands and thousands of soldiers had passed through there.

"And, what? You danced with GIs at the base?"

"Sure. There was a dance every Wednesday night. Most of the boys were there just waiting to ship out."

"How was that? I'll bet they were pretty frightened about going into the war."

"Oh no. At least they didn't seem to be frightened. They'd been trained. They were all in it together. But sometimes they would say they were a little worried about what would happen. You know men don't like to look soft."

"And you danced with them on Wednesday evenings?"

"Yes, and on Saturday nights we would go into town, and the Masons had a dance for GIs too. I think that was mostly for officers."

"So *two* nights a week you went to dances with soldiers who were headed for the European war? How long did you do that?"

"The whole time."

"And that was?"

"Three years."

Three years of dances twice a week!

"But that means you must have danced with hundreds of GIs, or maybe even ten times that many."

"Well, sure. I loved to dance. And dancing back then wasn't just reserved for sweethearts. Everybody danced with everybody. Not with the same person all night. It wasn't serious or anything."

"But … What I'm saying is that after they left Harrisburg they went straight over to Europe."

"Yes, they all said that's what was going to happen to them."

Did she see it?

"That's what I mean, Mrs. Musser, Ruth, did you realize that for many of those boys you quite possibly were the last woman they held before going into battle? And for some, maybe, you were the last woman they would *ever* hold?"

"Yes… I… I guess I knew that."

Of course she did. How could she not?

"Did you hear from any of them again?"

"Oh… A few of them would write. And I would write back to them, of course… And there was this one fellow… We wrote for quite a while. He went to somewhere in Italy and they were pinned down for a long time."

"Do you think he was at the infamous stalled invasion at Anzio?"

For the Allies in Europe, the battle at Anzio was exceeded in grim notoriety only by the Battle of the Bulge.

"Well, they couldn't say where they were, and all I sent mail to was an APO address."

"So what became of him?"

"His letters just stopped… I wrote, but nothing would come back."

Being neither kin, nor next of kin, she would not have been notified.

"I'm sorry to hear that. But you should be proud to have kept his spirits up—and all the other boys', too."

Ruth silently looked toward the window and the brilliant autumn sky beyond.

And Ruth Musser had done "nothing much" during the war.

I wrote the story. I gave Ruth a copy, then changed the names in it as I said I would and took it to my writing class. Now that

Mark Kramer was interested in my project, he decided that even though I was only auditing his class, he would read the story.

We sat down after the term was over and we talked.

"This is incredible," he said. "How did this go for you?"

"Well, I started off all wrong, in my nervousness forgetting everything you taught us about interviewing. But once I calmed down, I just let her talk and lead me into it. She kept saying she had never done anything important or exciting. But she loved to dance, and dancing references were scattered throughout what she told me."

I'd had enough writing classes by this time to know that instructors are careful to nurture creative neophytes. And I took Mark's words for that care, at least until he suggested that I try to get the piece published. I could see he was actually serious about my work. I'd not considered publication, and as I did, it seemed like too much of a stretch—a distraction from the hospice writing I was trying to get to. And at least as I thought about it then, publishing patient stories, almost certainly posthumously, did not fit in with what I wanted to do.

"Mark, I told [Ruth] it was only for this class. And she really seems to not want to talk about it too much. And I'm not interested in writing for magazines. That's a different sort of challenge. For that I could see interviewing her more and finding others like her. There should be someone somewhere who might want to talk about it a little more than she did. I suppose that if I worked at it, I might be able to get a little more emotion out of the interview. I guess I was a little embarrassed."

I thought for a moment then added what I really hoped to get out of writing others' stories. "The imagery she created in my mind was very poignant. Once a few details started to come, her voice changed—the look on her face as well. It was pretty obvious those GI dances had been important to her, even though she kept telling me how unimportant she was. I got caught up in her reminiscence, I guess you could say. We both were enjoying her recalling past people and adventures."

"But it did get a little surrealistic now and then. A couple of times I felt a little like a voyeur when she seemed to travel back. But once I got the hang of it, I was really pleased—to actually get into the feeling of her story, I mean. But, you know, the woman is the mother of a friend of mine, and I think that complicated how it went from both sides—maybe otherwise I would have pressed for more details. Or maybe she would have been more forthcoming. Every now and then I felt she was holding back, but I'd not press her. That's what I meant about not being a journalist—they always go for the story, don't they—no matter what?"

Mark nodded, then asked about the writing itself.

"I found it challenging trying to make a cogent story out of details that came over three interviews. And each one of those was pretty convoluted too. Deciding how to write it—how to make it interesting to a reader—was not easy, but when the pieces came together, I wrote it out in nothing flat. I really felt great when I delivered it to her. I'm pretty sure I'd done something for her that no one else ever had."

"And I remember you said this was sort of a pilot piece—a trial run?"

"Yes. I did this to see if I might be able to write stories for hospice patients. I'm a volunteer with the Good Samaritan Hospice. And what do you think about that idea, Mark?"

"Well, you seem to have learned a lot on technique just from this one instance. More importantly, how do *you* feel about it?"

"One thing's for sure, writing for them will be a little more challenging, and not only because they will be complete strangers when we start. I mean they are, after all…dying—may even be gone when others get to read their stories. I showed [Ruth's] story to the hospice volunteer coordinator, Anna Olszewski, and she got very excited. I think she hadn't realized that I was going to do anything this in-depth or create a story that was so lengthy. She called it a memoir. I think she is pleased. She said she was going to approach the hospice director about the idea of me writing for patients."

"Yes, but how do *you* feel about it?"

"Mark… I don't know… It just feels right somehow. And not only for me, but for the patients and their families too. I mean until I did it, I hadn't thought about what going through the interview process could be like from interviewee's point of view. On the whole, I think [Ruth] liked the experience, once I caught on how to handle the interview. And I hope hospice patients might have a similar reaction. I guess I'd not only be writing a story for others, their family mostly, but also I would be giving the patient a chance to reflect on the whole arc of life they led. You know, some retrospective—on the fullness of their life. Maybe a sort of closure.

"And this kind of writing seems to appeal to me. I mean I get to do the writing and put all of the effort into making the story into a good one, but it is not about me. Maybe that has to do with all the technical writing I've done. I'm most comfortable writing about something other than myself. To try to connect with the feeling of another person, though. Wow. And then to try to convey the same feeling to the reader, that would be some challenge."

"'Challenge,' you use that word a lot. I think you should go for it.

"And here's one more challenge, Richard. If you do decide to go through with this, there is one other story you ought to consider. Your own. Keep notes. Maybe you'll want to write about the whole experience some day."

A Writing Partner's Tale: *Pain*

In the face of pain, there are no heroes.
George Orwell

Rose Mondell was by far the most challenging person I have written for as a volunteer for Good Samaritan Hospice. In fact, interviewing her was so troubling that I sought professional help.

I met my friend Dr. Tod Marion for breakfast at a Denny's in Cranberry, Pennsylvania. I'd warned him on the phone that I needed a little guidance about Rose. Tod said he would listen. I had already spent more than six hours talking with Rose by then, and I was frustrated.

Tod is a professional geriatric psychologist. I asked for and got his promise of confidentiality. So over our coffees, I gave him the story of Rose's life.

Apart from the facts of Rose's stories, I also described her emotionless way of telling them—stories bitter, often sarcastic, yet delivered in a bland, flat monotone. Rose's body language was always tightly closed, and her face frozen with no hint of emotion. Although she freely shared her stories, everything except her words conveyed an isolation beyond standoffish. Her words were haunting, wrenching and often bitter, and they seemed to issue from a fortress, even when Rose described the most terribly traumatic events of her life.

As our bacon and eggs were set before us, I put down my coffee and looked pointedly across the table at Tod.

"Well, what do you think?"

Tod has always encouraged me in my volunteer work writing hospice patient memoirs, so I knew he'd help if he could.

With the briefest of pauses, he spoke: "Classic rejection reaction. That's what most of her stories are about, really. Rejection. She had to cope, so she's built a shell, a wall. Maybe even she herself is the only one allowed inside."

Mentally, I ran through my experiences with Rose. Tod's observations made sense, since no one could have started life with such an attitude. It had to be the product of environment, her upbringing. And for sure rejection certainly characterized much of that.

"Do you think I have any hope of getting at least a look inside her fortress? Her memoir is going to be very dark and very dry unless I can get some sort of emotion out of her."

Tod studied his plate. "Since she may have been hardening her shell for her whole life, you may not stand much of a chance. I know she is in hospice care, but I'd say that if she wasn't so near her end, she probably should be seeing someone. It's very possible she is in a deep, deep depression."

I slumped and took a long sip of my coffee. "Can you suggest anything that might help me out? Something I might do to get her to give me a little of how she feels about the things she tells me?"

"Probably nothing you haven't already done. Provide positive feedback—encouragement through reinforcement. Bonding. Reflection. Sympathy. I'm sure you're listening right, from what you've told me. Apart from your just being empathetic, I'm afraid it will just have to take time."

"I'm not sure how much time she has, Tod. Rose is dying of complications from a stroke. I guess it's the complications more than the stroke itself, since she's not paralyzed. She's given up, or as the hospice write-ups describe it when someone just wants to stop living, 'failure to thrive.' Even over the weeks I've visited her, I've noticed a decline—slowing of replies, weakening of voice, decreased activity. She's not disinterested, though. It's more a sort of winding down."

"Maybe there is something else," Tod said. "If you can get her to talk about things or events she really enjoyed, that might give you some new insight or even get her talking. Might help her attitude during the discussion. That's not much. I wish I could give you more help."

"Maybe I can use that," I told him. "Rejection. I will see what happens if I start openly talking about rejection and how it affected her. And about getting into some happier memories. Maybe I can come up with something she's already told me that could be a focal point for that kind of discussion."

At the cash register, we settled our bills, I thanked Tod, and we parted.

My mind churning, I made my way down the highway. Halfway home, Tod's suggestion sparked the whisper of a single word Rose had mentioned. Maybe there was something that I could try after all. I sped up.

* * *

I'd told Tod about Rose Mondell's harsh childhood, followed by a hasty, teenage marriage that ended with an acrimonious divorce. And that divorce happened back when the word carried a lot more baggage than it does today. Back then it was an indictment.

Her mother had died when Rose Williams was a baby. So in 1925 Robert Williams, her father, decided to put his four children into the Protestant Orphan Asylum, on a hill across the Allegheny River from Pittsburgh. To him the orphanage seemed the best option to keep Jean, Barbara, Marlene, and Rose together. The uncertain financial times and Robert's need to be at work during the day had fueled his decision, as Rose explained it to me. For Robert, the Protestant Orphan Asylum seemed the wisest choice— the girls would be together, they would be properly cared for, and he could visit them. Moreover, unlike giving them up for adoption, he could get his girls back when he was able to care for them again. All in all, to him it seemed like a logical solution for a man who no longer had a wife. Even so, I wondered how he could do it, entrust his own daughters up to strangers. They were just children. And baby Rose, the youngest, was barely two years old.

As it happened, some of the things Robert assumed about the orphanage were not to be. First among them was that the girls would be together. The orphanage separated children not only by sex, but also by age, so two-year-old baby Rose rarely got the support of her older sisters' company.

Then there was the matter of the quality of the care. It ran the gamut from Miss Bollan, a warm nurturer who enjoyed children and was good to them, to Miss Mason, a cold disciplinarian to whom the orphanage seemed little more than a paycheck.

Of course, even the best caregiver cannot replace a mother's love. And baby Rose hadn't had much of a chance to experience that in the first place.

Telling me this, Rose brought it home by recounting her grandson's reflection on the loss of his mother. Rose's daughter-in-law had succumbed to cancer. Flatly, without the emotional overtone that almost anyone would give to such words, Rose said, "Reed told me, 'She wasn't just my mother. She was my best friend.' I'd never thought about it like that." And who could expect her to, bereft of a mother of her own? Hearing this, I was moved to tears by the thought of someone never knowing a mother's love. But Rose looked more puzzled by the thought than saddened by it. I jotted a note that it was not until her grandson told her about his loss that Rose seemed to consider her own.

More troubling yet was that the molding influence orphanage life had on Rose Williams was not always so passive. The first thing that Rose told me about was the stigma that accompanied living in an orphanage in the 1920s. The children were given severe haircuts by whoever was available, and so their Spartan heads marked them for all to see. Their clothing was just as conspicuous. They had to wear drab uniforms—the only clothes they had—even to the public school they walked to each morning.

The school nearest the Protestant Orphan Asylum was Clayton Elementary, and it was there that Rose began to understand she was different from other students. For that difference, Rose was bullied. Today, we have extended the word "bullying" to include verbal abuse. In Rose's time, however, this word was reserved for things more physical. When she told me she'd attended a public school, I sensed there might have been trouble.

"I guess the other students probably gave you kids from the orphanage a hard time, picked on you."

Rose snorted. "It was not only the students, but the teachers. If anything went missing, the first ones they took back into the cloakroom were the kids that came from the home. That's who they figured stole it. The teacher would take us back there and 'frisk' us. That's the nicest way I can put it."

"Why do you say it that way? What happened back there?"

"I learned that if I said I didn't do something, that meant to them that I did it. So I never said anything. Because if they'd asked me, and I said no, they'd send me into the cloakroom to be stripped.

"Degrading. Sometimes the teacher did it and sometimes they had some of the students do it. They really looked down their noses at us, and we knew it too."

"Strip searches of schoolchildren. Incredible."

"Just for the ones from the home. I never saw any of the other children get stripped," she grimly replied.

"How did that make you feel? I mean it must have made you feel really bad about yourself."

"Probably, but eventually it got to the point where the next one accusing me of anything was going to pay dearly for that. That was what I did. If I was going to be stripped, they were going to pay."

"You learned that you had to take care of yourself, Rose."

I got only silence in reply, so I continued. "You must have had to play with the other school children. What happened there?"

Rose was being bullied, but she in no way allowed herself to become a victim. She had her own desires and the drive to pursue them. In the late 1920s, when women had only recently been granted the right to vote, and little girls were still expected to only play with dolls, Rose asserted her way into an exclusively male pastime.

Back when The Babe was knocking them over the center field wall at Yankee Stadium, what Rose Williams most loved to play was not dolls, but baseball. And she was going to play no matter what.

"I had to play with the boys but I was bigger than them, back then. Once they saw I was serious, it was, 'Show us what you can do,' and I don't remember what I showed them, but whatever it was it must have been pretty good, because I passed [my tryout]. I got to play on the team. I was the only girl."

"Did you play any particular position?"

"I was the pitcher. And I pitched because I was the best. We played on a real ball field, too. And since I was the only girl on the team, the other teams would laugh, but when I'd strike a few of 'em out, then they wouldn't laugh so much."

I thought back to my own elementary school childhood. Like most boys of the 1950s, I had played baseball when I could—whenever and wherever we could get enough fellows together. We got on a real ball field only if the older boys in the neighborhood were finished with it. Otherwise, we'd just use any grassy plot. There was definitely a pecking order.

But pitcher?

That was always a revered position. When there were enough kids to have two teams, I had *never* been the pitcher. That position was always reserved for the very best players, the athletes, the ones who would go on to be called "jocks" in high school. There was plainly another pecking order within the pecking order of age. And even though as a child I'd played some thirty years after Rose's time, I cannot recall there ever being even one girl on a baseball field with me—in any position.

Yet Rose had not only been playing baseball with boys, she had been their pitcher!

I tried to think of just how formidable a girl would have to be to have pitched with the boys that I grew up with—how capable and how assertive. Then I tried to imagine just how much *more* formidable she would have had to be thirty years earlier. It was beyond my imagination.

Amazed, I looked up from my notes at Rose in her cranked-up hospital-type bed. As always, her curly silver hair was probably primped just for my visit. She was withered and bedridden, but she still had her pride, her head held erect.

In that moment, only the *huff-chuff* of the oxygen machine filling the silence, Rose turned toward me. Our eyes locked, and in mine she saw that I fully understood the magnitude of her accomplishment—her *triumph*. Satisfied, she acknowledged my understanding with a curt nod and only the tiniest upturn at the corners of her mouth.

Outwardly, Rose dealt with being in "the home" through a stoic resolve suborned by aggression. But I came to feel that inwardly, things were even more troubling.

As Rose grew, she developed her own ways of dealing with the reality of daily existence at the Protestant Orphan Asylum, the only home she knew. Most likely, her ways were different from the other children's. But clearly Rose's behavior was the result of her certainty that it was up to her and her alone to deal with whatever situation might arise. As a result, Rose felt she was the equal of any and all challengers. As but one graphic example of her attitude, Rose described how she handled punishment for taking a shortcut.

"Taking a shortcut sounds pretty harmless. Why punish you?"

"It's worse than you think, so I'll try to remember the reason I did it in the first place … Cleaning. That was it. Every week we got a new duty. One week mine was cleaning the cook's bathroom. But when I'd finished, instead of going out through the door, I took a shortcut and jumped out through the window. And I got caught. And Miss Mason got really mad. Who knows why? And I got punished for it—whipped. She had a rod and she had tied it with leather strips, and she whipped me on my legs with it." A little girl, she wore a dress of course.

"And for such a little thing! Did you cry?"

I was hoping for some emotion in Rose's response.

But Rose replied in her characteristic deadpan: "I was not too happy."

The foundation of her toughness began to emerge. "So, I happened to know that she had a bad knee. And [in the dining room] we had these long tables with benches … And it dawned on me that I could get back at her, hurt her, with that table bench. So when she was walking by, I tipped the bench … And it came down, smashing her right on her knee." Quickly, just a hint of a smile. "And that put her in the hospital." Tiny smile disappearing just as quickly, she deadpanned: "For just for a little while, though."

Amazed, I asked, "Did you think you could actually get away with that?"

Almost casually, Rose explained the reality of life in the POA to me: "Oh, she always got even. They all always got even." She looked away, the matter now closed.

Not wanting to let it go, I said, "Did the other children in the orphanage do things like that too, too?"

"Oh, I knew I was different from the other kids. I grew up with the feeling that that was just my way of living. Kids didn't call me names or make fun of me like they did each other. Not too many, anyway. They knew I'd get back at 'em if they did.

"It was hard, but acceptable for me. But with others it was different."

"How so?"

"Well, we had our crybabies. I couldn't ever understand why they were crying all the time. The ones like me who came in when we were young, there wasn't anything to cry over. But some came in when they were older. Our crybabies were some of those. Now I know that was because of what they missed. But I never had what they had, so there was nothing for me to cry over.

"But back then, I just wanted them all to shut up. I wanted to box their ears."

A once-popular Pink Floyd recording verse popped into my head, and I jotted: *"Momma's gonna help build baby a wall."* I could see that without a momma, Rose had built an entire fortress all by herself.

As Rose finished the sixth grade, her father Robert finally felt he had the wherewithal to get his four girls out of the orphanage. Rose was now twelve years old. She had spent almost eleven years in the orphan asylum. It was the only way she knew of being, even as she moved into a more conventional family setting in a house with her father, her grandmother and her three older sisters.

I couldn't fathom why her grandmother had let her and her sisters go to the orphanage or why it had taken her father more than ten years to get them out again. But I made no comment, even though it crossed my mind that Roosevelt's New Deal had then been in full swing, including a hike in the personal income tax. Was her father thinking of the four girls' dependency deductions? Or perhaps had he gotten a better paying job in the improved economy that the New Deal brought? Rose made no comment on the length of time she and her sisters spent at the POA. Anxious to get beyond the darkness of the orphanage stories, I let the matter drop. I had no idea on how I would handle this in her memoir.

Rose did not tell me very much about the years she spent in her new family home, either. However there was one story she did tell about her life with her reconstituted family. It serves to illustrate that the years at the POA had already left an indelible mark on her not to be erased by the change to a more conventional family situation. Rose simply continued to assert her aggressive independence.

"I'll bet it was nice to have your sisters around again. How did things go?"

Rose snorted. "I never saw 'em. My sisters had boyfriends." Thinking back, she went on, "And they got gifts—candy.

"They all knew I had a sweet tooth, so they'd put their candy up in the closet. And after some of it had disappeared, then they thought to put a lock on the door. But I figured out that if you took the hinges off the door, you could get it open anyway and get the candy out. But they might check on it, so I put stones back in—little pebbles—so they could take the box out, rattle it, and put it back. They'd never know that I'd emptied it.

"It took them a while until they opened it, but they figured out right away what had happened and who had done it." Was that hint of pleasure in her voice?

Mark Twain once said, "The apple that is come by through art is always tastier than one gotten honestly." Was it that? Or was Rose relishing her triumph over her sisters? How her ways must have stressed the reunited Williams family household!

I wanted to ask about other, happier memories, but Rose was not interested in talking more about her reunited family. She wanted to move on—unfortunately to an even more distressing story.

Rose explained me that she decided to get married at age seventeen against her father's wishes. Not only was he opposed to her marriage at such a young age, but he vehemently disagreed with her choice of a husband as well.

Her family was solidly Presbyterian, but Rose wanted to marry a Catholic. In her day that was called a "mixed marriage," it then being unthinkable to marry someone of another race, a definition the term would carry decades later.

I said nothing of that, but asked: "So why did you want to get married, Rose?" I expected to get a story of young love. But, no.

"It was a spite marriage because of my father. I shouldn't have … My father was a very, very forgiving man. But he … How will I put it? He … He forgave you, but at the same time he didn't like it… He forgave you on one level but on another level, he didn't."

I'm no psychologist, but I got the real meaning. Rose was letting me know that her father was a hard man. Rose had spoken without emotion, but her careful searching for words devoid of it said a lot.

As to the marriage itself, given Rose's tales of the orphanage, I understood her way of reacting to authority—any authority. Fight or flight. Against her only parent, fight was off the table, so Rose acted simply to get out of his reach. If marriage was the only way to do that, then on with it. But I now knew better than to hope her story would brighten at this new departure.

"Just about the time the [Second World] war was getting started was the time I married that jerk, Joe. He worked for Acme window washing company, so at least he had a job of some kind. And I got two very nice children by him. He'd been my first boyfriend. I got married in a Catholic church so that he could continue in his Catholic ways. My father would not come into that church. And my husband had to sign a paper that said he was going to raise the kids Catholic because I would not convert. But I got married anyhow even though somebody else gave me away. I don't even remember who it was.

"Then Joe went off to the war. He went into the draft—right at the beginning of 1942. We got married in January, and Jan was born in November of 1941." Giving me these details was Rose's way of making certain that I understood that her marriage had been one of choice, not necessity.

Rose did not have much more to say about the war years. She had a job as a sales clerk, with her sisters watching her children when she was at work.

"What did you do about entertainment, Rose?" I asked, ever hopeful for some sort of emotive description.

"Well, I didn't want to leave the kids at night, so we'd sit and listen to the radio. Those old programs were funnier—better than TV, if you ask me. They were the best."

And from there, Rose jumped ahead to the end of the war. By that time she had had the second of her husband's children, Michael, whom she calls Mickey. Rose described her husband's homecoming from the war with considerable contempt. On that point, I'd have to agree with her.

"He came back after the war, all right, but it wasn't because of me. He'd left another woman here. I had no idea. But I'm sure lots of other people knew.

"One day I got a phone call—an actual girlfriend of mine. Her name was Rose too. She lived on the next block. She called up and wanted to know if I would send Joe down to help her with something. And she asked if I could watch her little daughter. I said, 'Yeah, sure' and I sent Joe down. Rose sent her daughter up for me to watch … Then her and Joe could go to bed. Nothing like having a built-in babysitter."

That was one of Rose's little attempts at humor—always dripping with sarcasm. I didn't laugh, and I'm not sure I was expected to. In the language of her day, *Rose was being two-timed.* Naturally, with attitude of active self-preservation, her Joe's philandering was not a topic for discussion between them. Instead, Rose left and got a divorce as soon as she could. She fought hard for, and got, custody of her two children as well.

As usual, Rose delivered all of this wrenching, revealing information flatly, so I once more tried to get some emotion out of her.

"Oh, Rose, how did you feel about that? You must have really been hurt."

"I felt mad—mad at me—that I would hurt the kids that way."

Mad at herself?

"I woke up one night and my daughter was sitting beside my bed—crying. I knew it was my fault. I think if I would have thought things out better, it might have been different. I might have done things different."

Surprised at her blaming herself, I said, "It doesn't sound to me like you were that cause of any of this. Looking back on it now, do you still think it was *your* fault?"

I expected neither the anger in her sharp reply nor her choice of target: "You want to know plainly how I see it now? That I was a stupid jackass. Oh, I can't help it now, I know. But I really was."

Is this what it looks like behind Rose's wall?

Rose still chided herself, even though her divorce was more than fifty years in her past, even though her husband was the obvious cause of it.

I made a few bone-headed moved myself as a teenager. Who hasn't? Of course I now understood that they were the doings of a young, immature version of myself. I've forgiven my younger self his mistakes. But it was clear that Rose Mondell would not, could not, do likewise, even now as she was now nearing the end of her life. How terrible.

I tried to sympathize: "Oh, Rose, I'm sorry that you had to go through all of that. And even after Joe was gone, I know that being divorced wasn't very well received back then. It must have been really hard. I remember my uncle married a divorced woman in the 1950s, and the whole family talked about 'that divorcee' like she was some kind of ..."

"Whore," Rose flatly interjected.

I felt deep sorrow for Rose and what she had been through simply because she had been born when she was. That she still carried such a low opinion of herself for what was, after all, the doing of an adolescent who had had to live through a horrendous childhood, was terrible. At a loss for what I could do to help, it was then that I'd resolved to see Dr. Tod Marion about Rose.

* * *

As I drove home from breakfast with Tod, a single word Rose had spoken came to me. Maybe there was hope for connecting with Rose. Tod had said to look for something that she said outright that she'd enjoyed.

When I got home, I replayed Rose's interview recordings. I remembered something that Rose said that she enjoyed. I was listening for the word *radio*.

It took a while, but I found it. Rose had mentioned evenings sitting in her living room with her children during the war. She'd said she really enjoyed listening to comedy on the radio.

Even though it was before my time, I am inclined toward nostalgia about the 1930s and '40s. Perhaps it was originally kindled by the black and white movies of that era—ones with Humphrey Bogart, Betty Davis, and the like. Or maybe it was the rich sounds of the big bands—Glenn Miller, Tommy Dorsey, and others. In the 1960s, I'd played in a semi-professional (we got paid) big band myself, so maybe my infatuation goes back to that.

I'm not sure exactly what created it or exactly when, but the warm feeling I have about that era is embodied in the image of the family gathered around their living room console radio.

TV does not evoke this in me. To me, TV is a much more lonely experience, dominating sight as well as sound. Then, too, in the era of radio, somehow life looked a less complicated and seemed more livable. Problems seemed to be more solvable. Even that era's own war, World War II, seemed more just and more clear-cut than those I've lived through—starting with the Cold War and continuing on to today's "war on terror."

Since my family has always known of my nostalgic streak, one Christmas years ago, I got a gift set of thirty audiocassette tapes. Each had shows broadcast in the '30s and '40s. The collection was called *The Golden Age of Radio*. I'd listened to them all at least once and to a few favorites several times. Since then, they'd been boxed and forgotten. Who plays audiocassettes any more?

Homing in on Rose's reminiscence about radio, I rummaged around in closets and the attic before finding the recordings in the basement, still packed away from our last move. They were boxed up along with our old vinyl record collection.

I inspected the assortment's index, and it all flooded back to me. I easily remembered the ones I'd liked the best—the funniest ones. I connected a PC to my audio system and played the selections I had remembered as the best ones: *Amos 'n' Andy, Jack Benny, Jimmy Durante,* and one that featured renditions of the top selling records of its day, *Your Hit Parade.* I transferred episodes of all of these and a few others onto a couple of CDs. I'd noticed that Rose had a radio/CD player next to her bed, and I was creating an audio time capsule to play on it.

I made a special trip out to deliver the recordings.

When I explained what I was giving her, Rose perked right up. She actually gave me a full smile. And her eyes widened as I described the details of what was on the CDs.

I put the first disc on her player and started it up. On came one of the *Amos 'n' Andy* programs. There they all were: Calhoun, The Kingfish, Lightnin', Sapphire, and of course Amos and Andy were narrating it all. Rose lit up. And I let out my breath.

"Oh, thank you! I haven't heard them in years and years. They were on TV for a while, but it wasn't as good the radio was. Thank you, thank you!"

"Well I'm glad I cheered you up, Rose. You've had me worried." People I work with show a visible lift when they get into telling their stories, but Rose hadn't. "There's a lot more programs on the discs. Enjoy yourself—I'll just leave the first one playing for you. No interview today. I'll see you next week." I don't think she even noticed I was leaving.

Smiling as I went down the stairs, I thought I heard Rose burst into laughter. I say "thought I heard" because since I'd known her, I'd never once heard her laugh before.

Jan, Rose's daughter and in whose house we were, met me at the bottom of the steps. As she had in the past, she asked, "Would you like a cup of coffee before you go?"

"Caffeine is always appreciated, Jan."

I sat down at the kitchen table. Jan took something from the oven.

"Fresh coffee *and* chocolate chip cookies—personal nirvana."

Perhaps overdone, but I tried to keep it light. Caregivers have enough to worry themselves already.

Jan seemed to have something on her mind. We sat sipping our coffees, and after the small talk, she expressed her concern. "Do you think you'll be able to finish in time?" She, too, had been noticing that her mother seemed to be weakening.

"I've been having some difficulty in getting any emotion at all out of your mother. It might be me, or maybe just the way she is."

"Well, now that you mention it, the only time in my life I've seen her get emotional or cry is at weddings or funerals. She keeps a pretty tight control of her emotions."

She lost her self-control once long ago, running off to get married. Was that it?

But it would be too embarrassing, too personal, to ask Jan this question, even though it certainly would explain a lot of Rose's need to control her emotions—even now at the final stage of her life.

When I returned for another interview, Rose told me a lot of stories about her life with her children. Mostly, they were about the holidays and her children. They were the sort of bemused stories most parents have about kids' antics. But there was one story of another sort.

Because it otherwise might appear that Rose Mondell was uncaring or hard-hearted, perhaps it will serve to illustrate that she was not. This story took place early in her second marriage, which didn't seem much more happy than her first, to hear her describe it—except for her children, of course. From this story, it's clear that although Rose was not much given to *display* warm, loving emotions, she definitely had them.

"In the neighborhood where we lived, my kids knew some children that were in foster homes. They would come over to play, and I would talk to them, sometimes. I think I knew a thing or two about what they were going through. I wanted to be someone they could talk to about it, you know? Nobody listens to kids, especially when they're not your own."

That was telling indeed. "What did they say to you, Rose?"

"That they were afraid. They didn't like where they lived. They said they wanted to come and live with my kids."

"Isn't that another way of saying that they wanted to come and live with *you?*"

"I guess so. They were just kids. They were going through a bad time in their lives, I knew. So I would talk to them. In fact it's been years, but all along I still hear from them. They write to me. They both live in Monroeville, but they are not related to each other. They still write to me."

"That must make you feel pretty good, doesn't it?"

"Well the world didn't come with instructions. I just use common sense."

Self-effacing, no matter what.

As I was nearing the end of my interviews with Rose, wrapping up so that I could start writing her memoir, I reminded her of something she'd said.

At the outset of working with a writing partner, I always ask whom they would like to read their memoir. Then I ask my writing partners to tell their stories to *them* instead of me. Sometimes it is easier for them to relate to people they know than to a volunteer from the hospice. Moreover, when I write their memoir, it's a great help to know who the audience is going to be.

Rose Mondell had been quick to say that she wanted her memoir to be for her four children.

So in our last interview I reminded her.

"Rose, we're just about done here. Since you want this to go to your children, is there anything else you'd like me to put in here?"

Rose thought for long seconds. Then she started with what seemed to be a story about something else entirely, but I let her go. "I met a doctor once, a couple of years back. I was sitting in his office waiting for my turn. When he finally came out, he said to me, 'Why do you look so glum, Rose?'

"I said, 'I don't know, Doc—I guess I just feel glum.'

"He said, 'Well, yes, you can't just look glum without feeling glum … Are you unhappy about something?'

"'No,' I said.

"Then he said, 'Well, then, don't you like yourself?'

"I said, 'No … I'm not my favorite person.'

"He said, 'Well, you should be.'

"So I asked him, 'Do you like yourself?'

"Then he said, 'I *love* myself. I can't wait to get up in the morning and get to work. Every day is great. That's how much I like myself.'"

Here, Rose paused.

"And that's what I'd like all my kids to do…"

I struggled to keep control, and asked softly, "Do you want me to put that in your memoir, Rose?"

I let the silence extend until Rose decided to fill it.

Looking pointedly at me, she said clearly, just as level as always: "Put that in there because that's what I'd like to tell them."

And I did. I put that story into the epilogue that I reserve for my reflections on working with my writing partner. There, too, I put my thoughts about Rose Mondell. I know that her children, all of whom I had met after one of the interviews just before Christmas, were hoping to gain some insight into their mother's self-effacement and her self-deprecating gallows humor, and I tried to give them some—at least from the perspective of a family outsider.

My epilogue had to do with words.

The dictionary defines the word *pragmatic* as "dealing with things sensibly and realistically in a way that is based on practical rather than theoretical or emotional considerations." When I wrote the epilogue to Rose's memoir, I used that word to describe her. But now, I wonder if *pragmatic* is what Rose really was. Maybe she went beyond what is the commonly understood meaning of that word. Maybe Rose took pragmatism to the extreme. So what is the best word for pragmatism taken to the extreme?

Some choices: hard-headed; hard-nosed; no-nonsense. I find none of these adequate in describing Rose Mondell.

Perhaps baby Rose had been born with something like a gene for pragmatism. Then she was swamped with rejection, as Dr. Marion had put it when I talked to him. This brew of nature and nurture had produced *something* in Rose. Unfortunately, that something has a lot of negative connotation. For me, the word that best describes what Rose had become at a very early point in life is *tough*.

She was resilient in dealing with her challenges, and she was certainly resourceful. These are components of toughness. In addition to her toughness, or perhaps because of it, Rose isolated herself.

Yes. Rose was both tough and isolated. But she was not unloving or cold.

I learned a valuable lesson from Rose Mondell. A virtue, when taken too far, becomes vice, a shortcoming. It can make you into something that you were not—something you would never consciously choose to be.

As I look back on it, I see that perhaps when Rose, who was approaching the end of her life said, "I'm not my favorite person," this is the reason. In toughing it out, in striving to wall off the rejections that she experienced, perhaps Rose also walled off a part of herself.

I do not for one second think that Rose Mondell, the least emotive person I've ever written for, was an unfeeling person. Rather, she was one who felt compelled to keep her emotions totally isolated from everyone, including her public self.

I wrote her memoir as best I could. Quite a bit of it consisted of recollections of holidays and special occasions spent with the four children her two husbands had given her. These were the most positive of her memories. Her children held the true light of life for Rose, and probably that was why she directed her memoir to them.

But I hope Rose Mondell's four children gained some insight into their mother, especially from the memoir's epilogue.

Being mindful that the *most* important audience I write for is my writing partner herself, I am never critical. The patient is why I'm writing in the first place, and I always respect that as well as the short time they have left.

After all, an important purpose of any memoir, including the one you're reading now, is to expose the inner character of the storyteller. And what I saw behind Rose Mondell's wall of toughness was not a stitch of hate, but an awful lot of pain. I hope that the memoir I wrote for her exposed that a little. Her children wanted to know about it, I think.

In our last meeting, I gave her the final copies of the completed memoir whose main text she had already read and approved. Upon reading my appended personal Epilogue for the first time, Rose Mondell looked up and simply said to me, "Thanks for saying what I couldn't."

Journey: Epilogue

In the quiet conversation that sometimes comes after I deliver the final copies of a writing partner's memoir, Marilynn Duff asked me a question I'd not been asked before.

"Why do you continue to do this writing work of yours? Yes, you told me how you got started. And, yes, you told me how you like to learn new things. But there are a lot of other ways to learn new things, and any of them would be a lot simpler than what we've done here."

For emphasis, as she was prone to do, Marilynn looked at me and narrowed her eyes.

Then she continued, and if only hearing her firm incisiveness, no one would ever guess she was 92 years old and in her last days.

"And yes, yes, of course I know you want to help me—maybe help me to face what I have to. But you could do that without the work of all this writing. Other hospice volunteers just show up for a visit once a week, but look at this thing."

Marilynn's memoir, entitled *Behind the Great Wall* to emphasize her pioneering visits to a just-opened China, had come in at more than 23,000 words.

Sensing that she thought something deeper was driving me, I looked carefully at her and paused. Was this a silent bonding moment? Was she hoping I'd get religious? What, exactly, did she want from me?

I scratched my cheek. Maybe I could try an analogy. Something she could identify with.

"You know, Marilynn, you've been all over the world. You are the most culturally experienced person I've ever known, so how about this? Although it didn't start out this way, maybe now I can say what my writing is like for me: It's sort of like going to an Indian lunch buffet." I stopped, gauging her reaction.

Her eyes widened. The non sequitur had her interest.

All right, then!

"There are all these strange dishes, and I can't imagine the taste of even one. They all have names, and if you go there for dinner, those names are listed on the menu—each followed by an English description. But words about tastes don't give much of a clue."

On a roll, now.

"But at the lunch buffet, I can see, and maybe smell, the dishes. I don't even read the names. On my first pass, I try this. Sample that. And on my second round, I go long on whatever I really liked. I go back till I've had my fill."

Is that amazement in her widening eyes?

I dug in deeper, bringing the analogy home.

"Isn't that just like when we drilled down into some of what you told me on our first visit? We picked out the dishes we liked. Then we savored a giant helping of each. And we wound up with a wonderful meal—your memoir!"

In high gear now, heading for a big finish.

"For me the flavor is always intense. And unexpected. Foreign. It's curry and coriander. A lot of tastes and aromas. And more and more till we've had enough. It's heavenly. You just can't get this kind of understanding from a book, or a movie, or even a class."

Satisfied with myself, I leaned back and looked at Marilynn in her cranked-up recliner. The only sounds were the hiss of her oxygen cannula and the huff-chuff of the machine feeding it.

Presently, her eyes narrowing again, came Marilynn's soft, stoic reply.

"Bullshit."

I exploded, spraying spittle with my guffaw. *Bullshit!* Laughter strangled me.

Impassive, Marilynn simply squinted on. But I could *not* stop.

At last her face crinkled as I'd seen it do many, many times. Then, satisfied that the friend I'd become got that she well understood *him*, Marilynn full-on cracked up herself.

We roared and gasped and laughed each other to tears.

Another unexpected vista along one more winding path of heart.

Notes and Resources

Notes

Except where noted otherwise, dialogue and quoted conversations with all hospice patients in this book have these sources: the final memoir written by the author for the patient and/or the audio recordings and written notes made at the interviews with that patient. There are no composite characters in this book.

Conversations with all others except hospice patients, except where present at a patient interview recording, is memoir.

All hospice patient interviews were conducted by the author from 2008 to 2017. As more than fifty interviews with patients of the Good Samaritan Hospice are the sources of this book and the memoirs written for the patients, the interviews are not individually cited below.

Lengthy direct excerpts from patient memoirs are denoted by indentation.

Dedication

Page v.   Epigraph: Opening quotation (in Spanish and English) to the Introduction of The Teachings of don Juan: A Yaqui Way of Knowledge, 40th anniversary edition, Carlos Castaneda, (New York, Washington Square Press, 2008), p.11.

Journey: Prologue

Page 7. First Hospice: Lynne Ann DeSpader and Albert Lee Strickland, The Last Dance: Encountering Death and Dying, (New York, McGraw Hill Education, 2010), page 192.

A Writing Partner's Tale: *Epiphany*

Page 19. Charlie Russell: Web site C.M. Russell Museum http:www.cmrussell.org.

Page 18. Yellowstone: US National Park Service web site at http://www.nps.gov/yell/index.htm.

A Writing Partner's Tale: *Bliss*

Page 55. Lao-Tzu: Tao Te Ching, Chapter 9, translated by Stephen Mitchell, (New York, Harper Perennial, 1988).

Journey: Finding Hospice

Page 91. The Five Wishes booklet is available online for inspection and downloading at a modest charge. It includes space for a will, a living will, a healthcare power of attorney, how you want to be treated if unable to communicate, and how you want to be remembered. The web site is: https://www.agingwithdignity.org.

A Writing Partner's Tale: *Courage*

Page 98. Mortality rates: Website Medical News Today citing Center for Disease Control statistics from 2014.

Page 108. Ice Bucket Challenge: Website of the ALS Association (http://www.alsa.org) accessed in December of 2014.

Page 108. Walk to Defeat: Winter Newsletter 2014, ALS Association of Western Pennsylvania

Journey: Evangelizing Hospice

Page 124. Camp Erin Pittsburgh is not unique. The Moyer Foundation has partnered with a number of other organizations to establish local Camp Erins for bereaved children. There are more than forty such camps around the country. Links to the website where locations of the camps can be found are on the author's web site, Writing the Memoirs of Hospice Patients, located at http://www.memoirwriter.org.

Journey: Epilogue

Pages 168-170. Excerpted from 2017 final interview notes for a writing partner written with in 2016.

Resources

Finding a Hospice, Learning about Hospice

The Hospice Foundation of America has an excellent website that is a good place to start as well as the National Hospice and Palliative Care Organization. Links to both can be found on the author's website, *Writing the Memoirs of Hospice Patients,* at http://www.memoirwriter.org.

Good Samaritan Hospice

As an example of what a good hospice might look like and could offer, take the link from the author's website.

Camp Erin for Bereaved Children

There are more than forty such camps around the country. They can be found at:

https://www.moyerfoundation.org/programs/camperin.aspx

Author's Website

There are more resources for those seeking information and understanding about hospice at the author's website, *Writing the Memoirs of Hospice Patients* which is located at http://www.memoirwriter.org. Additionally the site contains a blog where the author posts on items of interest to those seeking to know more about hospice. It is also and a place for those with friends or relatives who have died, or are dying, to share their thoughts, experiences and stories.

Writing Memoirs

There are Osher Lifelong Learning Institutes at more than one hundred universities around the country. They are learning communities for adults 50 and older and are funded in part by the Bernard Osher Foundation. The universities are listed at: http://www.osherfoundation.org. Additionally, there are many other such university adult learning programs available that are not underwritten by the Osher Foundation. Entrance to such programs does not require a college degree. Many, if not most, offer writing courses for those wanting to hone their skills.

There are also online communities that encourage memoir-type writing of all sorts. Many published authors blog about tools, tips and techniques for doing so. A good place to start is Sharon Lippincott's blog *The Heart and Craft of Life Story* at: www.heartandcraft.blogspot.com. On the first page are links to other writing blogs that you may wish to explore.

Also on the author's website, *Writing the Memoirs of Hospice Patients,* there is section devoted to resources for those wishing to undertake the writing of another's story. There is little in the wider world of writing about this topic specifically, so the author has posted the material he uses in teaching his ten-hour course on this topic. You can access the site at: http://www.memoirwriter.org. There is also a blog where the author continues to share experiences about writing in general and the capturing the stories of others in specific. Visitors are urged to post their own information and experiences as well.

Lastly, a workbook is available for prompting one through a process of recording a life's details and its stories. It is entitled *A Guide for Revealing and Telling Your Life Story.* The workbook is available for purchase from the Hospice Foundation of America. A link to this organization is on the author's website.

In instances where the author has not felt that he and a potential writing partner would be able to work together to successfully complete a memoir, he always leaves a copy of this workbook behind for loved ones to try to capture as much as they can.

Acknowledgements

This book is the culmination of considerable personal time spent with a number of hospice patients. While that is now obvious if you have read it, what may not be so obvious is just how many other people have also spent time with me in living the stories in *Paths of Heart*. More to the point, I have many, many debts of gratitude to repay.

Ruth Musser was a crucial person in the creation of my way of working, and so of doing the writing that is the basis of this book, as I have set out in the Dedication.

Mark Kramer also was a key person in my beginning the kind of writing I do. Apart from the things I picked up in his nonfiction writing class at the University of Pittsburgh, Mark not only gave me the nudge to try the first story, but also the encouragement to proceed to the next, and even to consider writing something like this book.

But really the first notion of creating the individual memoirs upon which this book is based came one afternoon while sitting in the office of the Volunteer Coordinator of the Good Samaritan Hospice, Anna Olszewski. Through suggesting it, then enabling it, Anna Olszewski is perhaps the person who most influenced this writing. Without her there would be no book because there would not be the memoirs on which it is based. That would be a true loss—for the patients and their families to be sure, but for me as well.

When Anna retired from the Good Samaritan Hospice, she was succeeded by Erin Middleton who performs that same function there. Erin saw fit to let me continue the memoir writing volunteerism that Anna enabled. Moreover, the hospice has added other volunteers doing similar writing work as well.

Also from the Good Samaritan Hospice, I would like to acknowledge Anzie Kelley, the Director whose approval and concurrence was necessary to start the project. Her successor, Judy Connelly, has given the same. In addition to these administrators, of course, there are the many caregivers at GSH who helped in the selection and screening of candidates. While there are always more than one hundred patients in GSH care, not all of them are able to, or may even want to, undertake this kind of work, so screening is essential. I could only emotionally handle the writing of one memoir at a time so the selection of which patient's story to work on next was particularly critical. Finally for spiritual advice, I would like to thank Pastor Paul, the Reverend Paul Rist, the GSH minister who meets the spiritual need of patients and staff alike in this emotionally difficult line of work. And finally, I owe a special debt to the former Hospice Unit director, Dianna Meade who was key in my discovery of the nature of hospice and people who make it what it is.

All of the proceeds from the sale of this book are being donated to the Good Samaritan Hospice itself—part of the Lutheran Concordia Ministries of Western Pennsylvania. If the effort put forth in the writing of this book is to garner something more than its own reward, the bounty is most deserved by that institution which so steadily strives only to ease our last steps in life.

And, I would like to thank those who enabled me to write in the first place. I must acknowledge with very deep appreciation those who, like Mark Kramer, were instrumental in turning an engineer and product manager into a writer. These are the people who teach writing and who administer the Osher Lifelong Learning Institute at the University of Pittsburgh. That program is partially underwritten by the Bernard Osher Foundation and is one of many at more than one hundred universities around the country. I am sure that there are many Osher students across the land who share my gratitude to Mr. Osher and the Foundation for what the program has meant for us. At Pitt, the program was begun by and ably headed by Judi Bobenage, Director, until her retirement. Judi's excellent beginning has been continued on by the equally able Jennifer Engel. And they both would tell you they ascribe a lot of the program's success to their right-hand woman, Patricia Szczepanski, Program Administrator. Because of these women, many, many adults in the Pittsburgh region have enjoyed a variety of informal classes at Pitt as well as the privilege of auditing undergraduate university courses.

Additionally, Sharon Lippincott was especially influential in convincing me that I could not only write this book, my memoir of writing memoirs, but also that I could get it published. Our hope for this book is that others might get interested in and attempt to capture and write the stories of those not inclined, or maybe not able, to do so. Sharon is a whirlwind of a woman and writing memoir is what she is about. If you Google her, you will find that she is a major player in the community of life story writers. What you won't discover in doing that, however, is the role she played in the writing of this book. The several OLLI classes she taught at Pitt gave me some of the writing technique for both the book as well as the memoirs on which it is based, but Sharon herself gave me much more than that. She helped to shape the book and as a critical reader early on was crucial in getting the tone and content straight. She does this for a lot of local writers in our area and with the aid of the Internet, well beyond. She is a treasure to those of us who had had the good fortune to know her.

I would also like to acknowledge psychological comprehension help given to me by Dr. Tod Marion. Tod is a friend who consulted with me on several hospice memoir projects. As a geriatric psychologist, his insights were particularly valuable in getting to core issues in several instances. Further, his encouragement that I write not only stories for patients, but also my own story helped to precipitate the writing of this book.

Finally, no writer should be without a competent editor, and I have been lucky enough to have two. Christine Stroud patiently edited this book, and shepherded it through substantial changes that got the can of worms under control. Christine is many things I am not, and so, she was able to show me a host of issues I had not even noticed, much less appreciated. And Laura Brown also edited the book, this at a crucial time when I decided to turn it inside out. It once was simply a series of essays with my own story a footnote.

I am lucky to have had all this help from all these people. Should you choose to give writing others' stories a try, you'll find there are those who will be glad to help you as well.

And that's simply because it's so easy to see capturing others' stories as a worthy endeavor—as a path that has heart.

About the Author

For more than a decade, Richard Haverlack has been writing the memoirs of others—more than thirty of them—penning somewhere between 500,000 and 1,000,000 words.

As a volunteer for the Good Samaritan Hospice, Richard works with patients to capture and craft compelling and sometimes poignant stories they want to tell others. Some leave these as life stories for their families, legacies for the future. Others take the opportunity to give heartfelt advice, frequently to children of grandchildren. And many simply have delightful stories they want *everybody* to hear.

But no matter what the motivation of the patient, their nearness to their ends works to bring forth stories that range from heartbreaking to astounding. And quite frequently, these stories surround kernels of meaning that we all can appreciate—lessons learned that we can all benefit from.

Richard has a number of degrees, but those are not what brought him to do the story writing that he does. Working with people to bring forth *their* stories is a unique and uniquely rewarding skill he has built simply because there were no "how to" references. Then, to help others to discover how meaningful and outright enjoyable it can be to write the story of another, he developed a course which he has taught at the university level.

Additionally, Richard speaks as an advocate for hospice in the hope that others will come to understand the benefits of it before personal situations force their hands. He does this because he himself had to scramble to find and understand hospice when his uncle at last arrived at life's end. Richard now does whatever he can to help others to avoid the confusion and anguish he and his uncle unnecessarily endured simply because they were unaware of what hospice does and why.

For more information, visit Richard's Facebook page or his website: http://www.memoirwriter.org.

74675390R00112

Made in the USA
San Bernardino, CA
19 April 2018